C000049476

TWELVE WORDS JESUS KNEW

Twelve Words Jesus Knew

IRENE LIPSON

MONARCH
BOOKS

First published by Monarch Books 1998

ISBN 1 85424 425 6

Editiorial Office: Monarch Books,
Broadway House, The Broadway, Crowborough,
East Sussex TN6 1HQ

British Library Cataloguing Data
A catalogue record for this book is available
from the British Library.

Designed and produced for the publishers by
Bookprint Creative Services
P.O. Box 827, BN21 3YJ, England
Printed in Great Britain.

To the memory of my dear husband Eric,
who taught me to respect the traditions of his people,
and who encouraged me to write this book. In accordance
with his wishes, I have made free use of his notes and
writings, many published in various periodicals and
many unpublished.

Zecher Tzaddikim Liv'rachah:
The Remembrance of Righteous Ones Continues to Bless

ACKNOWLEDGEMENTS

I would like to thank Walter Riggans for his encouragement and advice (mostly taken!), for finding the time to read through the manuscript and for correcting the most glaring errors and spelling mistakes.

Thanks are due also to Peter Simpson for generously sharing as much of his computer expertise as I was capable of absorbing.

My children–Andrew, Susannah, Joanna and Daniel–have been trying to persuade me to put pen to paper for years. Thank you for believing in me.

CONTENTS

בְּרִית

The bush blazed; God saying, 'I'm here!' The shepherd, startled, curious, drew near to examine this phenomenon. Then God spoke, recalling him to his responsibilities, abandoned so many years before. Questions were answered, doubts resolved, faith renewed, direction affirmed. Moses, with his wife and son, set out on the journey back. Surely all would now be well. But then, suddenly, at a wayside inn, disaster struck. Zipporah it was who understood. Her husband was being reminded of a crucial responsibility he had failed to meet. How could Moses represent the covenant God to the covenant people and to Pharaoh when he himself had defaulted as a father in Israel? Since the time of Abraham, fathers had been commanded to circumcise their sons as a sign of God's covenant between himself and his people (Genesis 17:11). And now God was about to 'remember' and reaffirm that covenant (Exodus 6:4–5). Apparently Moses had not remembered. How could Moses proclaim God's covenant renewal, having failed to bring his own son into that covenant–to celebrate the *Berith Milah* (the covenant of circumcision)?

1

BERITH

ברית

The Jewish Encyclopedia gives a triple definition of 'covenant': 1) An agreement between two contracting parties, originally sealed with blood; 2) A bond, or a law; 3) A permanent religious dispensation. Jakob Jocz[1] took a deeply theological view, writing that 'the basic Biblical category out of which all theological concepts arise . . . is the covenant relationship between God and man'.[2] This, he says, is a *living* relationship. Plaut[3] stated that the concept of 'covenant' expresses a context of mutual trust and obligation,[4] while Rabbi Louis Jacobs[5] said, 'The only true principle of the Jewish faith is that God has made a covenant with His people.'[6] This covenant is the basis and core of Israel's relationship with God.

There were, in the ancient world, two kinds of covenant. One was an arrangement, mutually agreed, between two parties of equal status (*syntheke* in the Greek); there would often be the eating of a meal together, including bread and salt, at the ratification of such a covenant. Responsibilities and benefits would be mutual. The other kind of covenant was a dispensation laid down by the stronger party, to be accepted or rejected, but not altered, by the weaker party (*diatheke* in Greek). Customarily the terms for such a covenant would be set out in a pattern: 1) The identity and deeds of the first party; 2) The promises of the first party; 3) The identity and responsibilities of the second party; 4) The identity (again) of the first party. In either case, terms were binding on both parties, and violation by either resulted in annulment of the covenant relationship.

A covenant was often sealed with blood. The expression 'to cut a covenant' arises from this (there is even a similarity between the Hebrew *berith* (covenant) and *barah* (to cut). The writer to the Hebrews (chapter 9) said that this made the covenant like a will, in that it required a death in order to be activated. The biblical concept of 'covenant' seems not to have fitted exactly into either of these categories. It is certainly more like the latter, but the conditional element is not the same. God, of course, will never be unfaithful to his covenant. The people surely will–and they will suffer for it. The current generation may cease to enjoy its privileges, but Israel will never, says God repeatedly, cease to be his people.

The theme of 'covenant' is like 'a gold thread of thought that gleams through Tanach (the Old Testament)– Pentateuch, Prophets and Writings–God's covenant faithfulness and love. "He keeps covenant love to a thousand generations" (Exodus 20:6)'.[7] Sometimes the benefits of covenant seem to 'leap-frog' over unfaithful generations to their more obedient descendants. Repentant sinners may always be restored into this relationship.

The covenant with Noah

Genesis 9 tells how, after the flood, God made a covenant with Noah and his descendants, and therefore with all humankind. He pledged to preserve the order of life on earth for all generations. This was an unconditional commitment on God's part. Men and women were required to 'preserve and show due regard for all human life'[8] but this was not made a condition of the covenant. The Rabbis have always regarded this, the 'Noachic covenant', as God's blueprint for the laws of all humanity. It may have been the guiding principle of the decisions reached by the Council at Jerusalem (Acts 15).

The covenant with Abraham

In Genesis 15 we read that God made a covenant with Abraham, subsequently confirmed in Genesis 17. This covenant was based on God's desire to bless all people on earth (Genesis 12:2–3). God stated his name, his deeds and his promises. This covenant was 'cut' (Genesis 15:10). Abraham was promised a seed, a land, a future, a relationship with God. All these promises were unconditional. The response required of him was circumcision. This was to be the 'sign' of the covenant. Chief Rabbi Hertz[9] said, on Genesis 17:2, 'What follows is not a compact between God and the patriarch, but a statement of the plans which He had designed for Abraham and his descendants.'[10] Plaut commented, 'Not only has He created a physical universe with immutable laws, He has established conditions for an unchanging spiritual world as well. God shows Himself, in the covenant between the pieces, to be a God who is both dependable and trustworthy.'[11]

So both these ancient covenants, with all humankind and then with the descendants of Abraham specifically, were unconditional. It follows that an unconditional covenant cannot be annulled unless the primary party is unfaithful. The faithfulness or otherwise of the second party is not relevant in such a case. Jocz said, 'The idea of a conditionless covenant is an innovation . . . behind it is the supposition of the utter faithfulness of the God of Israel.'[12] This is what makes biblical covenant unique. It *cannot* be broken by men and women, and it *will not* be broken by God.

The covenant with Israel

When God spoke with Moses, he made it clear that the action he was going to take on behalf of Israel was within the context of his covenant with Abraham. 'I am the God of your father, the God of Abraham, the God of Isaac and the God of Jacob' he says by way of introduction (Exodus 3:6); and 'I have remembered my covenant' (Exodus 6:5). In this development, Israel's covenant relationship with God would be based on what he was about to do, in delivering them from slavery in Egypt. That is why the Passover is so central to Jewish life. 'You shall tell your children,' he commanded them (Exodus 10:2; 13:8,14). These further promises associated with the exodus from Egypt (Exodus 6:6–8) are remembered today in the drinking of the four cups of wine at the *Seder* (Passover celebration): 'I will bring you out . . . I will free you . . . I will redeem you . . . I will take you as my own people.' And ever afterwards God would be known as 'The Lord your God, who brought you up out of the land of Egypt, out of the house of bondage'.

For Israel, the covenant God is the God who is *with* them. As he said in later, darker years: 'I am with you . . . this is what I "covenanted" with you when you came out of Egypt. And my Spirit remains among you. Do not fear' (Haggai 2:4–5). These words of covenant comfort were echoed by Jesus as he prepared his disciples for the coming separation: 'The Spirit of truth . . . will be in you . . . I will come to you . . . Do not let your hearts be troubled and do not be afraid' (John 14:17,18,27). This was a development, not an annulment, of the earlier covenant with Abraham.

But this time, far heavier demands were to be made by way of response. And those demands were presented at Sinai. Chief Rabbi Hertz said, 'Without the covenant at Sinai, the Exodus would have had little meaning . . . With the covenant at Sinai, everlasting life was planted in Israel's soul; and the story of Israel issues in eternity.'[13] As Jocz put it: 'Covenant . . . in the case of Israel, meant submission to the overlordship of JHVH and the acceptance of Mosaic law.'[14] *Torah*–the whole of God's 'direction' given to Israel at Sinai–was to be no 'optional extra', but an essential part of the covenant itself. To quote Jocz again: 'Torah is the token and pledge of Israel's special position as God's chosen people. *Torah* and covenant are inextricably linked.'[15] The covenant people is the people of the book–the people who respond, 'We will do everything the Lord has said' (Exodus 19:8).

Later covenants were subsequently entered into–with the Aaronic priesthood (Numbers 25:12)–a covenant of peace; and with the Davidic monarchy (2 Samuel 7:13,16)– a throne for ever. Strangely, it seems, the gold thread reached a high point at the nadir of Israel's story–in the prophecies of Ezekiel (37:24–28) and Jeremiah (31:31–34). The promise of the New Covenant is that there will be a lasting, fundamental change–*Torah* will be written on men and women's hearts. So will the promise of Deuteronomy 30:6 be fulfilled: 'The Lord your God will circumcise your hearts and the hearts of your descendants, so that you may love him with all your heart and with all your soul, and live.'

Signs of the covenant

The Rabbis recognise two 'signs' of the covenant: circumcision and *Shabbat* (Sabbath); although Friedlander[16] speaks of three more–*tzitzit* (fringes), *tefillin* (phylacteries) and *mezuzot* (portions of the Scripture fixed to the doors).[17]

Circumcision (Genesis 17:11)

This is so important that it is sometimes called, simply, '*Berith*'. In the *Talmud* it is also designated '*beritho shel Avraham avinu*' (the covenant with our father Abraham).[18] Plaut said, 'Few, if any, Jewish practices are more significant than 'Berith Milah', the covenant of circumcision . . . it confirms [the Jew's] special relationship to God.'[19] And *A Rabbinic Anthology* states that 'the law of circumcision annuls the Sabbath'[20]; that is to say, the *Berith Milah* must be done on the eighth day, even if that is *Shabbat*. The *Zohar* even goes so far as to say, 'As long as Israel observes the custom of circumcision, heaven and earth will go on their appointed courses, but if Israel neglects the covenant, heaven and earth are disturbed.'[21] Bearing in mind the importance attached to this rite, it is not surprising that the *Midrash* (commentary) on Exodus 4:24–26 says, 'So great is the command to circumcise that Moses, who neglected it for a single hour, courted death, and all his other merits availed him nothing.'

More recently, Chief Rabbi Hertz said, 'The rite of circumcision is the abiding symbol of the consecration of the children of Abraham to the God of Abraham.' This speaks of the whole people, but Hirsch[22] related it to the individual also when he said, 'The mohel (the official circumcisor) proclaims the full significance of the sealing of the covenant, which consecrates the whole human being to God . . . the living God becomes our only God.'[23] That is why, at the *Berith Milah*, the prayer is said, 'As he has been entered into the covenant, may he be introduced to the study of Torah, to the nuptial canopy, and to good deeds.'[24] There is a recognition that membership of this covenant community carries responsibilities as well as privileges.

Circumcision is not just a matter of the flesh. It symbolises total commitment to the God of Israel, who has chosen to commit himself to his people in relationship. Perhaps the spiritual meaning of circumcision is that of 'unblocking'; hence the analogy of circumcised hearts (Deuteronomy 10:16; Jeremiah 4:4) and circumcised ears (Acts 7:51). God looks for hearts and ears free to receive, respond to and share his love and mercy. The physical act alone is not sufficient. A relationship has been entered into. So the child is sometimes given the title 'bridegroom of blood', which inevitably recalls the incident in the life of Moses with which this chapter opened.

Shabbat (Exodus 31:13–17)

This is second only to circumcision as a sign of the covenant. It was given to Israel as a sign that God has made her holy, separate, different from all other nations (Ezekiel 20:12). Friedlander described *Shabbat* as 'An everlasting covenant and a sign between God and the children of Israel for ever.'[25] Rabbi Akiba[26] even understood the term *berith* itself to mean the observance of *Shabbat* and the recognition of God.[27] *Shabbat*, known as the 'Queen of festivals', stands very high indeed in Israel's order of priorities. Truly it has been said that Judaism is characterised by three things: circumcision, *Shabbat* and *Torah*.

The New Covenant

The New Covenant promises of Jeremiah 31:31–33, read in the context of the whole of chapters 31–33, clearly relate in the first place to God's covenant people, Israel. The permanence of God's relationship with Israel is compared with his relationship with the whole of creation. This is reminiscent of the terms of the Noachic covenant. Jeremiah 31:35–36 couldn't be plainer: 'This is what the Lord says, he who appoints the sun to shine by day, who decrees the moon and stars to shine by night, who stirs up the sea so that its waves roar–the Lord Almighty is his Name: "Only if these decrees vanish from my sight," declares the Lord, "will the descendants of Israel ever cease to be a nation before me."'

Freedman[28] pointed out that, as it was unthinkable for these natural orders to cease, so it is beyond thought that Israel would be completely and finally rejected by God.[29] But he stressed the mutuality of the relationship: 'The implication is that God will be what he has always been in his relationship to Israel; they, on the other hand, will now likewise permanently acknowledge him and be his people. Permanence is the essence of the new covenant.' And *The Jewish Encyclopedia* says of Jeremiah 33:25: 'God made a covenant with heaven and earth to observe the rules of day and night . . . Eternal as the covenant with heaven and earth is God's covenant with the seed of Jacob.'

The promise that God would write his law upon his people's hearts is surely as profound as any teaching in the Hebrew Scriptures; it calls to mind Moses' comment at the renewal of the covenant in Moab, prior to entering the promised land: 'But to this day the Lord has not given you a mind that understands or eyes that see or ears that hear' (Deuteronomy 29:4). Even Israel, chosen, loved, taught, shaped and guided, is unable to respond appropriately in covenant relationship with a holy God. So God himself will step in, at some time in the future, to make whole this relationship which is so near his heart; 'They–my people, I–their God'.

Messiah and the covenant

Malachi foretold that God would send the prophet Elijah as a forerunner of the Messiah (Malachi 4:5). This is to be seen as a renewing of the covenant. The expectation is acted out every year in the Passover *Seder* (order of service) as a cup of wine is filled for Elijah, the door opened, and there is earnest discussion among the children as to whether some of the wine has been drunk! The coming of Messiah is associated with Passover. But it is also remembered at the *Berith Milah* (circumcision). Elijah is said to be symbolically present at every *Berith Milah* in case the boy in question should turn out to be the Messiah. This is because every boy is potentially the Messiah. Elijah is so privileged, it is said, 'Because of his zeal for God's covenant in the days of Ahab' (1 Kings 19:10).[30]

Jocz stated categorically that the term 'New Covenant' is a Messianic concept. 'The "new" covenant,' he said, 'can only mean the "renewed" covenant, for the God of Israel is the God of renewal.'[31] This means that what is spoken of in the letter to the Hebrews (chapters 8–10) is not a break with the past but that Messianic renewal promised through Jeremiah. To think otherwise is to consider that God can make a mistake and have to start all over again; that God is capable of rejecting a people on the grounds of their faithlessness and failure: such a possibility casts a shadow over the character of God and over our own future as believers in Messiah Jesus, for we too are 'unprofitable servants'–faithless, failures. We are no more worthy than Israel that it should be said of us, 'God's gifts and his call are irrevocable' (Romans 11:29).

Jesus, of course, left his disciples with a startling visual interpretation of himself as the fulfilment of Jeremiah's New Covenant (Matthew 26:26–28; Luke 22:19–20). In a few short sentences during the Passover *Seder*, he revealed himself to be the fulfilment of the broken '*afikoman*'[32] seen mystically, in Jewish tradition, as 'he that is to come'; of the 'Cup of Redemption',[33] recalling the promise 'I will redeem you' (Exodus 6:6); and of the New Covenant, sealed with blood, as all covenants needed to be.

The implications of these words are mind-blowing. Here is a man, about to die a criminal's death, claiming–to all who know their Jewish Scriptures, history and tradition– that he is the promised Messiah, to be broken and to bleed in order to 'buy back' (the literal meaning of 'redeem'), not just the chosen few but 'many'; to bring to reality and perfection the covenant relationship as envisaged by Jeremiah. There is no negation of the promises to Israel; 'There is only one covenant,' said Jocz, 'In which the "new" covenant in the blood of Messiah is nothing else but a renewal of the "old"–that God wills to be present to his people.' But this covenant, with its promises of a changed nature, of full forgiveness and of 'knowing' God, is for 'all nations', according to the final commission (Matthew 28:19).

It would be wishful thinking and arrogance to claim that the terms of this New Covenant have been perfectly fulfilled at this time. We all know that our basic inclination is still to rebel against God, even though he has changed our hearts; that we still need to come continually for forgiveness, even though he has accepted us and made us clean; that we still do not 'know' God, in the complete, intimate, biblical sense of the word, as we would like, even though he has given us a knowledge of himself that we never had as unbelievers. The fact is that there is more still to anticipate. God has not yet finished. Surely, as Jocz said, 'The ingathering of the nations under the reign of God is the ultimate expression of covenantal grace.' God's ultimate goal reveals God's innate character: he is a God of *chesed*–of gracious, merciful, steadfast and faithful loving-kindness. Isaiah glimpsed it (Isaiah 11:6–9). John saw it on Patmos, and heard it too, in terms of the age-old covenant promises: 'Now the dwelling of God is with men, and he will live with them. They will be his people, and God himself will be with them and be their God' (Revelation 21:3).

Notes

1 Jakob Jocz. Hebrew Christian scholar of the middle years of this century. President of the International Hebrew Christian Alliance.
2 *The Covenant. A Theology of Human Destiny* (Eerdmans, 1968), p.19.
3 Rabbi W. Gunther Plaut, of the Union of American Hebrew Congregations.
4 *The Torah. A Modern Commentary* (The Union of American Hebrew Congregations, 1981), p.113.
5 Rabbi Dr Louis Jacobs. Rabbi of the New London Synagogue. Lecturer in *Talmud* at Leo Baeck College, London.
6 Rabbi Dr Louis Jacobs, *Theology in the Responsa* (Routledge and Kegan Paul, 1975), p.351.
7 Eric Lipson. Unpublished.
8 *The Jewish Encyclopedia*, vol. 4 (Funk and Wagnalls Co., 1903), p.319.
9 Dr J.H. Hertz. Chief Rabbi of Great Britain in the early years of this century.

10 *Commentary on Genesis* (Oxford University Press, 1929), p.145.

11 *The Torah. A Modern Commentary*, p.113.

12 *The Covenant. A Theology of Human Destiny*, p.27.

13 *Commentary on Exodus* (Oxford University Press, 1930), p.237.

14 *The Covenant. A Theology of Human Destiny*, p.21.

15 *Ibid.*, p.40.

16 Rabbi Michael Friedlander. Principal of Jews' College, London, at the beginning of the twentieth century.

17 *The Jewish Religion* (Shapiro, Vallentine and Co., 1922), p.335.

18 Avoth 3:17.

19 *The Torah. A Modern Commentary*, p.118.

20 *A Rabbinic Anthology* (Macmillan and Co., 1938), p.258.

21 The *Zohar* 1:93b.

22 Samson Raphael Hirsch. German rabbi of the nineteenth century.

23 Samson Raphael Hirsch, *Horeb*, 1837 (Soncino Press, fourth edition, 1981), p.535.

24 Singer, *The Authorised Jewish Prayer Book* (Eyre and Spottiswoode Ltd., 1957), p.305.

25 *The Jewish Religion*, p.335.

26 Akiba ben Joseph. First century. Sometimes called 'the father of Rabbinical Judaism'.

27 Mek. Yitro:1c.

28 Rabbi Dr H. Freedman.

29 *Commentary on Jeremiah* (Soncino Press, 1949), pp.212–213.

30 *A Rabbinic Anthology*, pp.256–257.

31 *The Covenant. A Theology of Human Destiny*, p.240.

32 The *Afikoman*, the broken piece of *matza* (unleavened bread), taken at the end of the Passover meal.

33 The third of four cups, recalling the promises of Exodus 6:6–8. Drunk after the Passover meal.

שבת

It was late afternoon one Friday in September. This was her first trip to Israel. It began in the usual way with the abrasiveness of the El Al 'inquisition' (understandable but nonetheless unnerving!); the altogether novel experience of being in the midst of what appeared to be a student reunion on the aeroplane; those few days at Emmanuel House, Jaffa– meeting the people and seeing the place I'd prayed for over so many years, exploring the artists' quarter, the tiny port; the anticipation and thrill of the drive up to Jerusalem. How high the walls were! Now here we were, showered and refreshed, on the roof of Christ Church, near the Jaffa Gate, in the Old City. What a view–and what peace as the Israeli working week wound down to its close.

Suddenly the peace was shattered by a loud siren. A child of the Second World War, my nerves jarred and I knew fear– yes, fear–again. Nobody had told me (why had nobody told me?). How should I know that the siren is sounded to alert people to the fact that the Sabbath will shortly begin? This was modern Israel welcoming in the Sabbath, the most significant moment of the week. The sound which for me was associated with black-out, bombs, V1s, V2s and that awful 'dug-out' at the end of the garden, here symbolised the very antithesis of these things: *Shabbat*–Queen of festivals.

2

SHABBAT

שבת

Sign of the covenant

Shabbat was to be a 'sign' between YHWH and Israel, an
everlasting covenant (Exodus 31:16–17). The *Talmud* says
that this means it is one of the 'signs of the Covenant'[1]
expressing, as *The Jewish Encyclopedia* puts it, 'the intimacy
between God and Israel'. This concept of *Shabbat* being an
expression of the special relationship which Israel has with
the Lord is what lies behind the unique place that the
seventh day has always had in the hearts of Jewish people.
As Maimonides[2] said, 'The Sabbath is a sign between the
Holy One, blessed be He! and us for ever.'[3] In a hazardous,
cruel and unpredictable world, *Shabbat* has been Israel's
refuge, hiding place and, together with circumcision and
Torah, her statement of identity. Hirsch[4] saw the weekly
keeping of *Shabbat* as a regular renewing of covenant relationship with God; a dedication of the individual to God's
service. In response, he said, 'On every Sabbath God will
give you renewed enlightenment of the spirit, enthusiasm
and strength for the fulfilment of the great task.'[5]

A memorial

God originally blessed the seventh day because that was
when he rested, or ceased, from his work of creation
(Genesis 2:2–3). At Sinai this was given as the reason for
Shabbat to be remembered and kept (Exodus 20:8–11).
When, years later, Moses reminded the people of the ten
'Words' (Commandments), he added another reason for
the memorial: 'Remember that you were slaves in Egypt
and that the Lord your God brought you out of there with
a mighty hand and an outstretched arm. Therefore the
Lord your God has commanded you to observe the
Sabbath day' (Deuteronomy 5:15). *Shabbat* is a memorial
both of creation and of redemption.

As the two Sabbath loaves are broken and shared, it is
customary for each family member to dip the portion in
salt. Salt is a sign of the covenant, a reminder of the
special relationship between God and Israel. The eating
of this bread and salt reaffirms individual and family
commitment and loyalty to the covenant God.

Shabbat is also associated with holiness. 'Observe [it] by
keeping it holy' (Exodus 20:8; Deuteronomy 5:12). God
himself made the day holy (Genesis 2:3). From this comes
the custom of welcoming *Shabbat* in with the drinking of
wine and the *Kiddush* service (the word *kiddush* derives
from *kadosh*–'holy'). Epstein[6] said that *Shabbat* should be
'a day to be devoted to holiness . . . free from all workaday
occupations, in order to have time to think of the ideas of
Holiness and of those beliefs without which Holiness, as
our religion understands it, can never be attained.'[7] So,
because holiness means separation, there must be a clear
demarcation between this day and all other days. The
beginning and the end of *Shabbat* used to be announced
by trumpet blasts.[8] Hence the siren that so startled me!

Nowadays *Shabbat* is welcomed in with the service of *Kiddush* and the lighting of candles. Its close is marked by the service of *Havdala*, where attention is drawn to the 'distinction between holy and profane; between light and darkness; between Israel, the recipient of Torah, and the other nations; . . . and between the seventh day with its joy, rest and peace and the six working days with their toil, rush and worry.'[9]

Remember, observe, honour, delight

The Rabbis teach that these four words are used in Scripture concerning the keeping of *Shabbat*: to *remember* means to greet the day with praise and with delight; to *observe* means to do no manner of work; to *honour* means to wear festival garments, welcoming the day as one would a king; to *delight* means to be joyful–as a symbol of this at least two candles are to be lit. There must be no fasting, weeping or grieving. Isaiah 58:13–14 is cited as authority here.

Remember

Shabbat recalls God's rest from creation and Israel's redemption from Egypt. Two loaves are on every *Shabbat* table as a reminder of the double portion of manna given by God on the sixth day, so that they should not gather on the seventh. But there are other reminders; every *Shabbat* recalls that God's people are to be holy. We can remember, too, the concept of 'rest' which is expanded in the teaching of Jesus (Matthew 11:28) and in Hebrews 3–4. So, with all the good things associated with this day, it is not surprising that Jewry should indeed greet *Shabbat* with praise and delight, singing, '*Shalom aleichem, malache ha sharet*':

'Peace be with you, you ministering angels.' A loved poem by Solomon Halevi Alkabetz[10] sums it up:

> Come, my beloved, with chorusing praise,
> Welcome the Sabbath Bride, Queen of the days.
> Sabbath, to welcome thee, joyous we haste;
> Fountain of blessing from ever thou wast,
> First in God's planning, tho' fashioned the last–
> Crown of His handiwork, chiefest of days.

Observe

The word *shabbat* means 'rest' or 'cease'. The idea is that work stops; not working is the essence of *Shabbat*. 'Rest and Holiness, Peace and Happiness, these are what must be the characteristics of the Sabbath,' wrote Basil Henriques.[11] The Rabbis have regarded work of any kind as a profanation of the holy day, even during ploughing and harvest (Exodus 34:21). So strictly was this commandment kept that, during the time of the Maccabean revolt, many Jews died rather than defend themselves by throwing stones on *Shabbat*; so Mattathias the priest ordered that it was legitimate to defend oneself if attacked (1 Macc.2:41). Even kindling of fire is forbidden. The *Mishnah*,[12] in fact, lists thirty-nine prohibited acts.[13] But *Shabbat* law can be set aside when life is in danger or a woman is in childbirth.[14]

Interestingly, 'rest' is not equated with 'inactivity'. Philo[15] said, 'Divine rest does not mean inactivity, but unlaboured energy.'[16] And, in our own generation, Chief Rabbi Jonathan Sacks[17] has said, 'The Sabbath cannot be construed as a day of leisure . . . in the modern sense of the word. Essentially it was a day of establishing alternative values.'[18] Dr Sacks is thinking particularly about the value of Jewish education–traditionally, *Shabbat* has been

seen as an opportunity for the study and the teaching of
Torah.

Honour

Shabbat has been called 'the Queen of festivals'. She is a
'queen', a 'bride',[19] a 'precious pearl'.[20] In Rabbinic times
'In honour of the Sabbath not only were the houses
cleaned and made bright and cheery, but they were also
decorated with myrtles. The members of the family bathed
and donned fresh garments.'[21] *Shabbat* is a royal guest;
preparations should be meticulous, everything of the best—
even the food! 'A heavenly gift . . . Shabbat is a beloved
guest. Complete rest, spiritual joy, serene contemplation,
devout prayer, congenial study, cleanliness, brightness,
best attire, festive meals, edifying conversation, overflowing parental and filial love'[22]; this was the ideal set before
the Jewish people by Dr Slotki, as they struggled to come
to terms with the post-Holocaust era.

I remember my husband telling this Talmudic story:
'Two angels, one good, the other evil, accompany every
Jew on Sabbath evening from the synagogue to the house.
If the Sabbath lamp is found lighted and the table spread,
the good angel prays that this may be the case also on the
following Sabbath, and the evil angel is compelled to say
"amen" to this; but if no preparations for the Sabbath are
seen, the evil angel pronounces a curse (may next Sabbath
be like this one), and the good angel is compelled to say
"amen"'.[23]

Delight

Ideally, Sabbath observance is to be a delight (Isaiah
58:13–14). 'Everyone in the synagogue turns towards the
door singing gladly, "Enter, O Bride."'[24] The *Talmud*
likens it to 'wholesome spices'.[25] The eleventh-century

poet Abraham Hakohen saw a picture of *Shabbat* in the simple narcissus: 'Saffron encircled by six petals, as the Sabbath is by the week-days.' As a symbol of this, Sabbath candles are lit, usually by the woman of the house, before darkness sets in. Far from being a day of dreary negatives and prohibitions, *Shabbat* has always been seen as a day of delight; its coming looked for with eager anticipation, its parting marked with regret but gratitude.

Any obligatory fasts happening to fall on *Shabbat*–with the exception of the Day of Atonement–are put off till the next day. Joy, rejoicing, are the order of the day. As *The Authorised Jewish Prayer Book* puts it, 'They will rejoice in Thy kingdom, all those who sanctify the Sabbath and call it a delight.' The picture of wholesome spices recurs in the *Havdala* service; a spice pot is passed round, and all sniff, as it were, the last traces of the fragrance of *Shabbat* as she is bid farewell for another week. And 'wine, when poured into a cup, is allowed to flow over, as a symbol of the overflowing Divine blessing which we wish and hope to enjoy in the coming week'.[26] Nothing must be allowed to vie with *Shabbat* for her place of honour and joy. So no weddings take place on that day–other celebrations may not adulterate *Shabbat* joy.

God's gift

To the outsider, *Shabbat* may seem to be a burden–the rules and limitations illogical and intolerable, but to the orthodox Jew through the ages it has seemed quite the reverse. There is a legend that explains this: on Sinai, after giving the third commandment

God then said to Israel, 'If you accept My Torah and observe My laws, I will give you for all eternity a thing most precious that I have in My possession.' 'And what,' replied Israel, 'is that precious thing which Thou wilt give us if we obey the Torah?' God: 'The future world.' Israel: 'But even in this world should we have a foretaste of that other.' God: 'The Sabbath will give you this foretaste. Be mindful of the Sabbath, to make it holy; be mindful of the promise I made to the Sabbath on the seventh day of the creation of the world.' For when the world was created, the seventh day came before God, and said to Him: 'All that Thou hast created is in couples, why not I?' Whereupon God replied, 'The community of Israel shall be thy spouse.' Of this promise that God had made to the seventh day, He reminded the people on Mt Sinai, when He gave them the fourth commandment, to keep the Sabbath holy.[27]

Shabbat is God's *gift* to Israel, a demonstration of his special love for her and a sign of his special relationship with her. It is an expression not of the unrelenting demands of a stern, forbidding God, but of the favour of a creative, liberating and sanctifying God; a gift–a precious gift from his treasury.[28] There is an ancient prayer that accompanies the *Kiddush* ceremony: 'In joy and favour Thou hast given us the holy Sabbath as a heritage, a reminder of Thy work of creation, first of our sacred days recalling our liberation from Egypt. Thou didst choose us from among the peoples and in Thy love and favour didst sanctify us in giving us the holy Sabbath as a joyous heritage.'

An oasis

Shabbat has been one of the most important factors in the preservation of the Jewish people: as a declaration of identity, but also as a relief which has made it possible to survive dynamically in an unremittingly harsh environment.

'The Sabbath was often a refreshing oasis in the desert of persecution.'[29] With the onset of *Shabbat*, it has been possible to escape–to discard one's troubles, anxieties, fears; to renew strength and powers of endurance; to rebuild faith and hope. Everything can–must–be put aside for twenty-five hours or so, and life acquires a mantle of beauty and peace. The Yiddish expression *Shabbasdik* describes the home which is suitably prepared on Friday evening to express all this. Chief Rabbi Sacks puts it most thoughtfully in these words: 'The Sabbath created the coherence of the religious community . . . It was, if you like, the insertion into the world of an alternative identity.'[30]

But this 'oasis' is not to be thought of as a means of escape from reality. It is more robust than that. It had as its object a hallowing of all life.[31] Heschel[32] taught that *Shabbat* was to be seen as 'a uniquely Jewish way to combat the dehumanising effects of rational, technological civilisation.'[33] And Grunfeld,[34] looking back to Deuteronomy 5:15, even went so far as to declare, 'Sabbath is a weekly recurring divine protest against slavery and oppression.' Israel is not meant to escape from the world but to be an active force for God within it; *Shabbat* has been given in order to make this possible. A Sabbath prayer, recently unearthed, of my late father-in-law[35] expresses this:

Almighty God, in thy goodness hast thou instituted the Sabbath as the day of rest for thy creatures. Thou hast ordained that on this holy day we should be free from the labours of the week, so that we may become refreshed and, with renewed vigour, enter upon the duties that each day has for us. Grant that this Sabbath be crowned with thy blessing and that each Sabbath day be a source of peace and of comfort. Guide us in the labours of the week. May thy Spirit be as the beacon of light pointing out the way of rectitude and righteousness. As week succeeds week, so may we be influenced for good towards all with whom we come into contact . . . We beseech thee, almighty Father, to cause peace to dwell in our midst, and teach us to find our highest good in thee. Amen.

A foretaste

The *Talmud* teaches that the ethos of *Shabbat* is 'a foretaste of the world to come'.[36] Philo taught that the future life would be an enjoyment of peace and rest in unblemished perfection. Jewry has always looked to the establishment of peace, justice and tranquillity as the accompaniment of the Messianic kingdom, after the pattern of Isaiah 9:7 and 65:25. *Shabbat* keeps this promise before our eyes, reminding us that today's darkness is not the final word; 'Sabbath symbolises the eternal Sabbath to come . . . symbol of the joy and peace associated with the coming Kingdom of God.'[37]

The soul of Judaism

As long ago as the time of the Maccabees, *Shabbat* became significant politically as a mark which distinguished the faithful from the half-hearted.[38] It is almost the 'Here I stand, I can do no other' of Judaism, both as religion and as identity. The ancient Rabbis even called *Shabbat*, *Yesod Haemunah*–the very foundation of the faith. As Grunfeld put it, 'Sabbath epitomises the whole of Judaism.' Not that everything but *Shabbat* is unimportant–rather, that *Shabbat* embraces everything else. Let *Shabbat* go and what is left? Basil Henriques stated categorically, 'This weekly festival is the most precious inheritance of the Jews. If it is lost, Judaism will be lost.'

So the emancipation of the Jews, beginning in nineteenth-century Western Europe, has not been seen as an unmixed blessing in the eyes of the Rabbis. When a Jew 'makes progress' in the secular world, the observance of *Shabbat* has too often been the first casualty, leading to loss of identity not only in the eyes of the world but even to himself. Grunfeld perceived this back in the post-war years, and wrote concerning the emancipation of the Jews: 'They gained riches . . . and, for a short while, political freedom. But they lost the Sabbath and with it the soul of our people.'[39]

The perception is, therefore, that 'the Jewish people stands or falls with the Sabbath'[40]; that it is by the keeping of *Shabbat* that Jewry has been preserved when so many other peoples have disappeared, swallowed up in the twists and turns of history.

Shabbat has been clung to, almost as a raft in a stormy sea; the only means of survival. If all else fails, *Shabbat* must continue. And so, over the centuries, this teaching recurs: 'The law of the Sabbath is equal to all the other laws and commandments in the Torah'[41]; 'The Sabbath is as important as all other mitzvot[42] combined'.[43] And the source of this importance has always been the appointment of God. The *Talmud* tells of a Roman governor who once asked Rabbi Akiba,[44] 'What is this day you call the Sabbath more than any other day?' The Rabbi responded, 'What art thou more than any other person?' 'I am superior to others,' he replied, 'because the emperor has appointed me governor over them.' Then said Akiba, 'The Lord our God, who is greater than your emperor, has appointed the Sabbath day to be holier than the other days.'

Biblically, *Shabbat* heads the list of the holy seasons (Leviticus 23). And so it stands pre-eminent; honoured, loved, enjoyed; truly the 'Queen of festivals'; the 'Bride'. Isaac Luria[45] expressed all that *Shabbat* is to Jewry in these words:

This day is for Israel light and rejoicing,
A Sabbath of rest,
When the work of the worlds in their wonder was finished,
Thou madest this day to be holy and blest,
And those heavy-laden find safety and stillness,
A Sabbath of rest.
This day is for Israel light and rejoicing,
A Sabbath of rest.

Shabbat Shalom

'*Shalom*', the customary Jewish greeting, acquires special meaning in association with *Shabbat*. When, in the hours before and during *Shabbat*, we say '*Shabbat Shalom*' to one another, we are expressing the hope that Almighty God will bless us with all the concepts that we have looked at in this chapter: that there may be an absence of persecution, illness, deprivation and, in their place, a sense of well-being. We have in mind the freedom to enjoy festive meals, tranquil family life, stimulating conversation. We think of the joy of fellowship in the synagogue, with its social intercourse. There will be the opportunity to renew strength in the study of Torah and the contemplation of holiness; to *enjoy* being Jewish in company with others of like mind and background. Hope may be renewed that one day things will be better. All this will pour into the troubled, sometimes frightened, soul the powers of resilience needed to tolerate and survive in an intolerable, destructive environment.

Shabbat rest

The word *Shabbat* means 'rest' or 'cessation'. The *Shabbat* laws all stem from God's desire that on this one day in seven there should be respite from the labour of other days. And so one should be free from the need to earn or provide a living, from the preoccupations of everyday life. This is the negative meaning of 'rest'. The positive aspect of '*Shabbat* rest' is that on this day one has time to engage in godly activities: in the study of *Torah* and, always allied to this, the *discussion* of *Torah* which, to the orthodox Jew, is never a burdensome duty but always a delight. One has time for prayer and meditation. There will be lengthy and leisurely worship both in synagogue and at home.

Family relationships may be developed and enjoyed, and children taught. Families will look for the opportunity to practise hospitality–no Jew should be alone or hungry on *Shabbat*, and it has traditionally been common for the man of the house to return from synagogue on Friday evening with an unexpected guest. Just as '*shalom*' is much more than absence of conflict, so 'rest'–*Shabbat*– is so very much more than absence of activity, than idleness.

'I will give you rest'

Jesus' teaching about *Shabbat* was robust. When the Pharisees jumped at the opportunity to condemn him for healing on *Shabbat*, he recalled them to the positive aspects of 'rest' (Mark 3:1–4). John tells us that on one occasion Jesus reminded them of a tradition that, for God, *Shabbat* has never ended–there being no words 'there was evening and there was morning–the seventh day' in the

Genesis account of creation (Genesis 2:2–3). The implication is that God is enjoying a perpetual *Shabbat*, and yet
he is engaged in the work not of creation but of sustaining
his creation. So, if even God is not idle on *Shabbat*, who
are they to condemn Jesus for 'working' (John 5:17)?

It is Matthew who gives us the essence of Jesus' teaching
on 'rest' (Matthew 11:28–30). The call is to the weary and
burdened: 'Come to me . . . and I will give you rest.' At
first sight this could be seen as a very attractive invitation
to escape from the harsh realities of life: 'Come to Jesus
and everything will be made easy'. But Jesus is in tune
with the best Rabbinic teaching that *Shabbat*-rest is more
than absence of toil. He goes on to say, 'Take my yoke
upon you . . . My yoke is easy and my burden is light.' The
'rest' that Jesus offers is not idleness and ease. It involves
the wearing of a yoke and the carrying of a burden. The
significance lies in the fact that the yoke is voluntarily
accepted from Jesus, who must have watched his father
make yokes that would fit the animal without chafing, so
that the work and the burden might be light. Jesus knows
the yoke that will fit me, and the burden that is appropriate for me personally. I am not to expect a life of total
relaxation, nor should I rush to take upon myself the
yokes and the burdens that others, or I myself, choose.
Wearing his yoke, carrying his burden; that is rest.

Entering God's rest

The letter to the Hebrews gives two chapters (3 and 4) to
the subject of *Shabbat*-rest. The writer was encouraging
the Hebrews to keep on, to 'hold firmly till the end' the
confidence with which they began their life in Messiah
(3:14). He reminded them of what happened to their
ancestors in the desert when they refused to enter the

promised land at Kadesh Barnea. God, he said, quoting Psalm 95:7–11, declared, 'They shall never enter My rest.' That generation never entered God's rest–that is, the land. The reasons for God's judgement are two: 1) a sinful, unbelieving heart (3:12), and 2) disobedience (4:11).

Now, what was this 'rest' to which God was leading his people? As we read the account of the conquest of the promised land under the leadership of Joshua, it becomes apparent that the experience was far from being 'restful' as we understand the word! They were called to a life of struggle, battle, hardship and labour as they ousted the current occupants, settled the land and learned to cultivate the vines and the fig trees under which they might sit. What kind of rest was this? Quite simply, it was the rest of being where God told them to be, at the time of his choosing, under his direction; the rest of trusting him implicitly in the most impossible of circumstances and, trusting, of acting in absolute obedience to his directions.

Shabbat–rest is what the people of God enjoy as we walk in covenant relationship with God, secure in his finished work of creation, of redemption; co-operating with his ongoing work of sanctification and of transforming the world; trusting him, obeying him; being what he wants us to be, doing what he wants us to do; in step with him.

Notes

1 Sanh.65b.
2 Moses Ben Maimon, or RaMBaM. Twelfth-century Talmudist, philsopher, astronomer and physician.
3 Moreh 2:31.
4 Samson Raphael Hirsch. German rabbi of the nineteenth century.

5 Samson Raphael Hirsch, *Horeb*, 1837 (Soncino Press, fourth edition, 1981), p.64.

6 Rabbi Dr Isidore Epstein. Principal of Jews' College, London, in the middle years of the twentieth century.

7 Rabbi Dr Isidore Epstein, *Step By Step in the Jewish Religion* (Soncino Press, 1958), p.100.

8 *Mishnah* Suk.5:5.

9 Rev. Dr I.W. Slotki. Principal of Manchester Talmud Torah School in the middle years of the twentieth century, *The Jewish Sabbath* (FOM Pub. Co. Ltd.), p.14.

10 Solomon Halevi Alkabetz. Sixteenth-century Cabbalist and liturgical poet of Safed.

11 Rev. Dr I.W. Slotki, *op cit*. Basil Henriques. Prominent lay member of the Jewish community in the middle years of the twentieth century.

12 *Mishnah*. Teaching, based on *Torah*, which was transmitted orally.

13 Shab.7:2.

14 Shab.18:3.

15 Jewish philosopher of Alexandria. First century.

16 *De Cherubim*.

17 Dr Jonathan Sacks. Chief Rabbi of the United Hebrew Congregations of the British Commonwealth.

18 Dr Jonathan Sacks, *Tradition in an Untraditional Age* (Vallentine, Mitchell, 1990), p.189.

19 Shab.119a.

20 Midr. Teh. to Psalm 92.

21 *The Sabbath* (The Joint Emergency Committee for Jewish Religious Education in Great Britain, 1943), p.6.

22 Rev. Dr I.W. Slotki, *op. cit.*, p.3.

23 Rabbi Jose ben Judah. Shab.119b.

24 Eric Lipson. Unpublished.

25 Shab.119a.

26 Rabbi Michael Friedlander, Principal of Jews' College, London, in the early twentieth century, *The Jewish Religion* (Shapiro, Vallentine and Co., 1922), p.344.

27 Louis Ginsberg, *Legends of the Bible* (Jewish Publication Society, 1992), p.386.

28 Shab.10b.

29 *The Jewish Encyclopedia* (Funk and Wagnalls Co., 1903).

30 Rabbi Dr Jonathan Sacks, *Tradition in an Untraditional Age*, p.195.

31 Rev. Dr A. Cohen, *Everyman's Talmud* (J.M. Dent and Sons Ltd., reprint 1937), p.165.

32 Abraham Joshua Heschel of Apt. Chassidic Master. Died 1825.

33 Arthur Green, *Jewish Spirituality* (SCM Press, 1988), p.426.

34 Dayan Dr I. Grunfeld, in *The Sabbath* (Jewish educational publication, 1943), p.9.

35 Rev. Solomon Lipson, senior Jewish chaplain to the forces, 1914–1918. Minister of the Hammersmith Synagogue, London, during the first half of the twentieth century.

36 Ber. 57b.

37 Rabbi Dr Isidore Epstein, *op. cit* (Soncino Press, 1958), p.104.

38 *The Jewish Encyclopedia*.

39 Dayan Dr I. Grunfeld, *op. cit*.

40 Rev. Dr J. Rabbinowitz in *ibid.*, p.7.

41 Yer. Ber. 3c.

42 *Mitzvot*: good deeds.

43 Rabbi Dr W. Gottlieb in Dayan Dr I. Grunfeld, *op. cit.*, p.24.

44 Akiba ben Joseph. First century. Sometimes called 'the father of Rabbinical Judaism'.

45 Isaac ben Solomon Ashkenazi Luria (ARI). Sixteenth-century mystic and teacher. Founder of the modern Kabbalah.

שְׁכִינָה

After my husband died, I found myself enveloped in a dark cloud, feeling a yawning emptiness within. This is an experience common to the bereaved, but it is terrifyingly isolating. I had no sense of that comfort of God so glibly spoken of by some who seemed to be living on another planet! For three months I simply clung objectively to God's faithfulness; to the promise that as I passed through this valley he would be with me. But comfort there was none. I felt myself stripped of personhood, significance; diminished; less than whole; dead, but still having to go on.

In this darkness I turned to the Psalms–where else?– crying, 'Lord, where is that sense of your closeness and your comfort that I was led to expect?'

Light broke through at last as I came to these words in Psalm 3: 'But you are a shield around me, O Lord; you bestow glory on me and lift up my head.' The worst was over. The long haul back had begun. God deals differently with each one of us in our times of darkness and need. This was his word for me.

So what does it mean for the Lord to be 'a shield around me' when I am so vulnerable? To 'bestow glory on me' when I feel so stripped of value? To 'lift up my head' when I am overwhelmed by the darkness? What is this 'shield'? What is this 'glory'?

3

SHECHINAH

שְׁכִינָה

'I have a dream!' Martin Luther King was a visionary and man of action who saw things as they were but also as they should be. A dreamer with the will and the drive to make the vision happen.

And God has his dream. He sees things as they are–himself marginalised and excluded; and as they could be–himself at the centre, living among and within his people, relevant to and significant in their lives. We hear it in the words 'and I will dwell among them' (Exodus 25:8). And we see it in the picture of the cloud and the fire in which the Lord went ahead as Israel came out of Egypt (Exodus 13:21). These words and this picture recur throughout the Bible. The Rabbis coined a word to describe the concept–*Shechinah*. The word doesn't occur in Scripture, though it comes from a Hebrew root which often occurs there. It is found in the two words *shachen*–'to dwell', and *mishchan*–'a tent'. *The Jewish Encyclopedia* gives two definitions for *Shechinah*: 1) literally, 'the dwelling', and 2) by usage, 'the majestic Presence or manifestation of God which has descended to dwell among men'.

In Jewish thought

Through the ages there have been those who have shared God's dream. The Baal Shem Tov[1] expressed this longing in these words: 'A man, wherever he is, or whatever he does, must concentrate his thoughts on the divine Presence, full of love for it, yearning for its love. And his recurrent thought must be: When shall I be worthy of the indwelling in me of the light of the divine Presence?' And the Lizensker Rabbi[2] promised: 'If your heart becomes pure, the Shechinah itself will sing within you.' *The Authorised Jewish Prayer Book* has this nightly prayer: 'On my four sides four angels, and above me the Shechinah of God.' And the hope for beyond this life is: 'Not like this world is the world to come. In the world to come there is neither eating nor drinking; nor procreation of children or business transactions; no envy or hatred or rivalry; but the righteous sit enthroned, their crowns on their heads, and enjoy the lustre of the Shechinah.'[3]

With Israel in the desert

As Moses was taking care of his father-in-law's flocks, 'the angel of the Lord appeared to him' and 'God spoke to him' from a burning bush (Exodus 3:2,4). The *Talmud* says, 'The Holy One, blessed be He, ignored all the fine trees and caused His Shechinah to alight upon a bush.'[4] The annotation to *Rashi*[5] says, 'God selected the thorn-bush, the lowliest of all trees . . . as a symbol that He was with the Israelites in their state of humility.' So here is *Shechinah*, seen as an angel, heard as God himself; a non-destructive fire; coming to the lowly, the despised, the undeserving.

As Israel came out of Egypt, the Lord went in front of them in a pillar of cloud by day and of fire by night (Exodus 13:21). As they crossed the Red Sea, the cloud moved from in front and went behind–light to Israel but darkness to the Egyptians (Exodus 14:19–20); he was both leading and protecting his people. At Sinai, 'there was thunder and lightning, with a thick cloud over the mountain, and a very loud trumpet blast' (Exodus 19:16), and when Moses went up the mountain to meet with God, 'the glory of the Lord settled on Mount Sinai . . . the cloud covered the mountain . . . the glory of the Lord looked like a consuming fire' (Exodus 24:15–17). Chief Rabbi Hertz[6] commented here that the cloud and the fire were 'the symbol and vehicle of the divine Presence'; 'symbols and witnesses to God's watching providence'. Here is *Shechinah*, defined in Jewish thought as 'the divine Presence', as cloud, fire, lightning; as sound–the voice of God himself; but also as glory–the glory of God. So God appears to his people, declares himself concerned about their situation, leads and protects them, talks to them and begins to show them what he is like. And the word we use to describe all this activity is *Shechinah*.

God threatened to withdraw his presence after the incident of the golden calf (Exodus 33:3), and Moses countered the threat by saying that the presence was the essential identification mark of God's people (Exodus 33:16). How could their claim to be God's people have any credibility unless the *Shechinah* was *seen* to be with them? Moses, having been allowed to see something of God's goodness and his glory (Exodus 33:19–23), himself reflected that same glory in his own face (Exodus 34:29). Maimonides[7] commented here that 'the glory of the Lord' is God himself. More is being revealed about *Shechinah* all the time: it can even be seen in the face of a person who keeps company with God.

After the tabernacle was built, 'the cloud covered the Tent of Meeting, and the glory of the Lord filled the tabernacle' (Exodus 40:34). Chief Rabbi Hertz commented: 'Exodus closes with the fulfilment of the promise, "There also I will meet with the Israelites. And the place will be consecrated to my glory . . . then I will dwell among the Israelites and be their God, who brought them out of Egypt so that I might dwell among them" (Exodus 29:43–45); and God's protective and sanctifying Presence in the midst of his people would lead them to their appointed destination.' This seems to be the first time that the *Shechinah* came actually *into the midst* of the people, and it was what God had envisaged from the beginning of the adventure–his dream ever since Eden. But when he comes there it is with demands and expectations as well as promises and blessings. He comes in order that his people may be consecrated to him, sanctified by him.

The Aaronic blessing

Aaron and his sons were told to bless the Israelites with these words: 'The Lord bless you and keep you; the Lord make his face shine upon you and be gracious to you; the Lord turn his face towards you and give you peace' (Numbers 6:22–27).

Chief Rabbi Hertz said of the Aaronic blessing, 'To cause the face to shine upon one is the Biblical idiom for "to be friendly to one" . . . it implies the outpouring of divine love and salvation.' The Rabbis have a beautiful rendering of this blessing: 'May He give thee the light of Shechinah; may the fire of prophecy burn in the souls of thy children; may the light of Torah[8] illumine thy house.'

God's 'face' and his 'presence' are the same word in Hebrew. When his presence–the *Shechinah*–is among his people, they will be walking in light and not darkness. Their innermost being, their whole personality, will be transformed. They will be living according to *Torah*– God's teaching, direction. And they will know *shalom*: peace which is not just absence of conflict, but wholeness and health in every department of life.

In the land of Israel

In the days of the prophet Isaiah, God's vision was far from being realised. In the first three chapters a picture is painted of failure, wilfulness, darkness; of vanity, arrogance, corruption, materialism, unfaithfulness. Then, in words surely designed to remind them of the days when *Shechinah* dwelt among them, the prophet sings of a future Messianic age, when God will finally, fully and permanently dwell in the midst of his people:

> In that day the Branch of the Lord will be beautiful and glorious, and the fruit of the land will be the pride and glory of the survivors in Israel. Those who are left in Zion, who remain in Jerusalem, will be called holy, all who are recorded among the living in Jerusalem. The Lord will wash away the filth of the women of Zion; He will cleanse the bloodstains from Jerusalem by a spirit of judgment and a spirit of fire. Then the Lord will create over all of Mount Zion and over those who assemble there a cloud of smoke by day and a glow of flaming fire by night; over all the glory will be a canopy. It will be a shelter and shade from the heat of the day, and a refuge and hiding place from the storm and rain.

> (Isaiah 4:2–6)

In exile from the land of Israel

If God's desire is to live among the people in the land of Israel, what happens when they are no longer there? This was a real problem for Israel during the long years of exile. How could they even worship God in a foreign land? And, in fact, Ezekiel saw in his vision the departure of the *Shechinah* from the Temple (Ezekiel 10:18–19)–as if *Shechinah* can take no pleasure being in the *place* without the *people*. But then, later, he saw the *Shechinah* returning (Ezekiel 43:1–5)–a symbol, surely, of the return of the people and the Lord to the land. *Shechinah* symbolises the presence of the Lord among his people, wherever they are. And Ezekiel closed his prophecy with words of rehabilitation, as he sees into the yet more distant future: 'And the name of the city from that time on will be "The Lord is there"' (Ezekiel 48:35). The fulfilment of God's own dream.

Back in the land

Zechariah, writing in the dismal reality of the return from exile, yet again lifted the people's eyes–heavy with disappointment and disillusionment–to the days when God would live in the midst of a renewed, enlarged, transformed Jerusalem. He used the familiar *Shechinah* picture: 'I Myself will be a wall of fire around it, and I will be its glory within' (Zechariah 2:5).

In Rabbinic tradition

Joseph Klausner[9] pointed out that in the first century CE,[10] awe of God's name led increasingly to an avoidance of saying the words '*Yahweh*', '*Adonai*', '*Elohim*'. Various other terms were used instead: 'Heaven'; 'The Holy One, blessed be He'; 'the Place' (*Ha Makom*); 'the Power'. Also two Aramaic words were used: *Yekara* (the Glory) and *Memra* (the Word). The term *Bath Qol* (the Voice) was used to represent God speaking intimately to his people. There was the term *Ma'mor*, defined by Klausner as 'the working instrument of Deity . . . an emanation of God Himself . . . mediating between the spiritual and material worlds . . . by which the world was created.'[11] The term *Shechinah* can perhaps be seen as part of this developing custom. Rather than use his name in a title like 'God's presence', one spoke of *Shechinah*, which is understood to mean the same thing. In fact Onkelos[12] used the word *Shechinah* to translate all the following terms: 'God', 'God's name', 'God's presence', 'God's face', 'God's glory', and 'God's holiness'.

Dr A. Cohen[13] went further. He said, 'Sometimes Ruach ha Kodesh (the Holy Spirit) seems to be identified with the Shechinah.'[14]

The Rabbis have had a problem with the identity of *Shechinah*. Is it sent by God? Or is it God himself? They have not been comfortable with the idea of God personally stepping onto the planet, so to speak. That might open the door to the concept of incarnation–which is unthinkable! And so Ibn Ezra[15] represents the more acceptable view, that 'The angel is not to be identified with God . . . He is here spoken of as God because he *represents* the Almighty'. Cohen attempts a reconciliation of the difficulty in words that remind one of the first chapter of the letter to the Hebrews: 'In the same way that the sun in the sky illumines with its rays every corner of the earth, so the Shechinah, the effulgence of God, may make its presence felt everywhere.' You can't look at the sun, say the Rabbis, but you can see its effect by looking at its rays; even so–you can't see God, but you see his effect by looking at *Shechinah*.

The *Talmud* teaches that 'when ten assemble for prayer, the Shechinah is in their midst; when three sit and judge, the Shechinah is in their midst; when two sit and occupy themselves with Torah, the Shechinah is in their midst'. And even when only one 'sits and occupies himself with Torah, the Shechinah is with him'.[16] Surely Jesus was thinking of such a saying when he promised his disciples, 'For where two or three come together in my name, there am I with them' (Matthew 18:20).

We have come to the point where inevitably our thoughts have been directed towards a more complete fulfilment of the *Shechinah* concept.

Shechinah and Messiah

The *Talmud* teaches that in the days of Messiah, when the tribes are reunited and the holy city restored, God 'will rebuild the Temple and cause his Shechinah to abide there'.[17] So a connection is seen between *Shechinah* and Messiah: Messiah will restore the people and the city, and rebuild the Temple; *Shechinah* will then come and live there. This reminds us of Isaiah 4. So Messiah and *Shechinah* are not the same, but they are closely linked. The separation of identity is necessary because in Jewish thought Messiah will be human only, not divine. God cannot be incarnate. Perhaps this is why *Shechinah* figures more in Jewish than in Christian thought, supplying the dimension of God presencing himself among his people. The connection is seen in some of the acknowledged Messianic prophecies, in references to 'light' (Isaiah 9:2) and 'glory' (Isaiah 60:1). Zechariah (father of John the Baptist) picks up the idea of 'peace' expressed in the

Aaronic blessing as he sings of the one who is to come and who will 'guide our feet into the path of peace' (Luke 1:78–79).

Shechinah was prominent at the most significant time of Israel's history–the redemption from Egypt. So if the coming of Jesus was significant, perhaps we should expect another flurry of *Shechinah* activity around the time of his birth and major life events. And that is exactly what we find.

Shechinah and Jesus

Surely what the shepherds saw in the fields on the night of Jesus' birth was nothing less than *Shechinah*; they saw an angel, the 'glory of the Lord', and they heard the promise of 'peace' (Luke 2:8–14). And they were terrified–just as Israel was at Sinai. At his baptism, the *Ruach ha Kodesh* (Holy Spirit) descended on Jesus visibly, and the 'voice of God' was heard (Matthew 3:17). When he was trans-figured, the three disciples saw 'glory', 'light' and 'cloud', and they heard the voice of God (Luke 9:28–36). Peter saw the connection, so he suggested building a *succah* (shelter) like Moses had when his face shone. But this was different– Jesus was totally suffused. Peter himself spoke in later years of this experience: he described what he saw as 'the Majestic Glory' (2 Peter 1:17).

As Edersheim[18] commented, 'The luminous cloud . . . is suggestive of the Presence of God, revealing yet concealing– a cloud, yet luminous.'[19] That same luminous cloud was seen at Jesus' ascension (Acts 1:9); that final, visual affirma-tion of who he was, coupled with the promise of a) the power of the *Ruach ha Kodesh* (Holy Spirit) and b) Jesus' own ultimate return in *Shechinah* glory. As he himself had promised: 'The Son of Man . . . when he comes in his glory and in the glory of the Father and of the holy angels' (Luke 9:26). We know that he is in that glory even now. Stephen saw him (Acts 7:56) and so did John (Revelation 1:12–16). Notice the familiar terms: voice, glory, light, fire.

In John's Gospel

John's introduction of Jesus is full of terms we now recognise: 'In the beginning was the *Word* [*Memra/Ma'mor*] . . . In him was life . . . the *light* . . . the world was *made through him* [remember *Shechinah* as the agent of creation?] . . . We have seen his *glory*' (John 1:1–14, my italics).

John was deeply conscious of the *glory* of Jesus. Recording the miracle at Cana he commented, Jesus 'thus revealed his glory' (John 2:11). Recalling the raising of Lazarus he noted Jesus' words, 'It is for God's glory so that God's Son may be glorified through it' (John 11:4). And it is John who remembered that Jesus spoke of his coming death as being 'glorified' (John 12:23), even as he had shared God's glory before creation (John 17:5).

In the letter to the Hebrews

Look at the way Jesus is presented at the beginning of this letter: 'his Son . . . through whom he made the universe . . . the radiance of God's glory'. The readers of this letter would immediately have seen the connection. *Shechinah* and Messiah are not the same, but there are common characteristics and functions.

Shechinah and Jesus' disciples

Jesus was concerned to share something of his glory with his disciples. He prayed for them as those to whom he had given of his own glory (John 7:22). Paul followed up this thought with these words: 'God . . . made his *light* shine in our hearts to give us the light of the knowledge of the *glory* of God in the *face* of [Messiah]' (2 Corinthians 4:6, my italics). And clearly addressing Gentile as well as Jewish believers, he spoke of '[Messiah] in you, the hope of *glory*' (Colossians 1:27).

Shechinah and the Holy Spirit

Shechinah was always a temporary presence. Jesus himself dwelt among humanity only for a while (John 1:14). But the coming of the Holy Spirit (*Ruach ha Kodesh*) was to be essentially different. God would give them 'another Counsellor to be with [them] *for ever*' (John 14:16, my italics). Not only *with*, but *in* them (John 14:17); not by any merit of their own but by relationship to the Messiah. Here is the answer to the longings of the Baal Shem Tov. Jesus linked this promise with the familiar word *shalom* (peace) (John 14:27). And with the fulfilment came the familiar form–fire (Acts 2:3).

The picture in the Hebrew Scriptures is of *Shechinah* coming upon and filling the tabernacle–and later the first Temple. This picture was taken up in Paul's writings, but with the Holy Spirit cited instead of *Shechinah*, and with the people as the Temple: 'You . . . are God's temple and God's Spirit lives in you' (1 Corinthians 3:16); 'Your body is a temple of the Holy Spirit' (1 Corinthians 6:19); 'We are the temple of the living God. As God has said: "I will live with them and walk among them, and I will be their God, and they will be my people"' (2 Corinthians 6:16). Why did God go to such lengths to redeem us? Surely so that he might live among us as a people, and within us as individuals. That is his longing still. And there is an ultimate plan, spelt out in the final chapters of the Bible: 'Now the dwelling of God is with men, and he will live with them. They will be his people, and God himself will be with them and be their God' (Revelation 21:3).

The heart of God reaches out to you and to me with the same yearning he has felt since the fall of humankind. He has never given up on us, and he never will. He wants to live within and among us; he wants to enjoy relationship with us; he wants to transform us and make us holy–with a holiness like his own.

We can hide from this destiny, feeling threatened and afraid, just as Israel did when they saw *Shechinah* reflected in the face of Moses (Exodus 34:30), and just as Adam did in the garden, having something to hide. But God's desire has not changed down the ages. He looks for a people who will expose themselves completely to him, welcoming him into their midst: living in his shadow, resting under his shelter; following the light of life; welcoming Jesus the Messiah into the centre; totally open to him, to the fire, with nothing to hide, nothing to fear.

> A fire that devours fire; a fire that burns in things dry and moist; a fire that glows amid snow and ice . . . a fire that is, and never expires; a fire that shines and roars; a fire that blazes and sparkles . . . a fire that burns without wood; a fire that renews itself every day . . . a fire that billows like palm branches.[20]

Notes

1 Baal Shem Tov: Israel B. Eliezer. Commonly known as 'Besht'. c.1700–1760. The founder of Chassidism, a sect which sought to escape from the dry, academic asceticism of current Talmudic Judaism. He taught that God is present

in all areas of life, may be worshipped with enthusiasm and joy, and experienced with devotion, love and piety.

2 Lizensker Rabbi: Elimelech of Lizensk. 1717–1787. One of the early 'masters' of Chassidism.

3 *Talmud*, Berachot 17a.

4 *Talmud*. Sot. 5a.

5 Rashi: Solomon Bar Isaac. French commentator on Bible and *Talmud*. 1040–1105. Commentary on Exodus edited by Dr A.M. Silberman.

6 Chief Rabbi Hertz: Dr J.H. Hertz. Chief Rabbi of the United Hebrew Congregations of the British Empire earlier in the twentieth century. Commentary on Exodus published 1930.

7 Maimonides: Moses Ben Maimon (RaMBaM). Talmudist, philosopher, astronomer, physician. Born Spain 1135, died Egypt 1204.

8 *Torah*: Primarily the five books of Moses (Pentateuch); the wide meaning is God's 'teaching' or 'direction'.

9 Dr Joseph Klausner. Writer, historian, Zionist. Regarded early this century as the authoritative Jewish nationalist historian. Wrote *Jesus of Nazareth*, 1907.

10 CE: Christian Era. Used by Jewish writers in place of Anno Domini.

11 Dr Joseph Klausner, *Jesus of Nazareth* (George Allen and Unwin Ltd., 1925), pp.196–197.

12 Onkelos. Convert to Judaism, late first century. Translated the Pentateuch into Aramaic.

13 Rev. Dr A. Cohen.

14 Rev. Dr A. Cohen '*Everyman's Talmud*' (J.M. Dent and Sons Ltd., reprint 1937), p.48.

15 Ibn Ezra: Abraham Ben Meir. Scholar and writer. 1092/3–1167. He has been described as 'the last of the great men who formed the pride of Spanish Judaism'. His chief work was a commentary on the Pentateuch.

16 *Talmud*. Ber. 6a.

17 *Talmud*. The *Midrash* (interpretation) to Cant.4:4.

18 Alfred Edersheim. Jewish Christian theologian of the latter part of the nineteenth century.

19 *The Life and Times of Jesus the Messiah* (1883) vol.2, book 4, chapter 1.

20 *The Celestial Fire.* Yannai. Sixth century.

'She's a wrong'un, Lord.'

'Yes, I know.'

'But you told me to marry her.'

'Yes, I did.'

'I shall have to get rid of her.'

'No!'

'But. . . .'

'Take her back; love her again.'

'But she's made fool of me . . . They titter as I pass by.'

'It's hard, I know. I know.'

'How can I take her back? I don't feel that I could ever. . . .'

'Who said anything about *feeling*?'

'But that's what love is–feeling.'

'So you think I *felt* like loving your people after they made that golden calf? You think I always *feel* like loving you?'

'No-o, I suppose not–when you put it like that.'

'Hosea, my son, I want you to do this. So that my people will know what love really is. I want you to pour love on this woman who is utterly unworthy; who will betray you again and again. One day I will give them an even better picture: then you will understand. Do this for me, Hosea–show them the meaning of my unfailing, loyal, steadfast love. My loving-kindness. My *chesed*.'

4

CHESED

חֶסֶד

Chesed (pronounced khēsed) is one of the richest and most precious words in the Hebrew Scriptures (Old Testament), for it goes to the heart of the character of God himself. It does not mean, simply, 'love'–there is another word for that. It is more an outworking of love–love in action, as the demonstration of a loving personality. There is really no single English word that can adequately translate *chesed*. The Authorised Version usually rendered it as 'lovingkindness' or 'mercy'; the NIV prefers 'unfailing love', and this is better, for *chesed* is a covenant word with a dimension of commitment whatever the cost. The Lexicon defines it as 'kindness; God's lovingkindness in condescending to the needs of his creatures'.[1] It often appears together with *rachmanuth* (compassion); 'together they describe God's tender mercy and loving compassion. These two words of the Bible are always in the background, ready to upstage fears and anger, mitigate punishment, express the fatherly-motherly love of God.'[2]

Rabbinic tradition has it that, according to Scripture, everything has been created by God's *chesed*: the world itself (Psalm 136:6)[3]; the heavens (Psalm 136:5); the throne of God himself (Isaiah 16:5)[4]. This makes sense because, say the Rabbis, God has himself said that he is the personification of love.[5] What he *is* and what he *does* will always be consistent, and this is particularly true in the case of *chesed*, because within that word are contained overtones of both character and actions. *Chesed* is active love. Rabbi Jonathan Magonet brings this out in his comment on Psalm 145. He sees God's *attribute* of *chesed* in verse 8 ('The Lord is gracious and compassionate, slow to anger and rich in [*chesed*]'), and his *actions* of *chesed* in verse 17 ('The Lord is righteous in all his ways and [*chasid*] towards all he has made').[6] 'Feeling alone is insufficient. To it must be added the willing heart that persuades us to do what is pleasing to God. Not saying but doing is the chief thing.'[7]

God's *chesed* for Israel

Chesed lies at the root of the Lord's dealings with Israel. This was recognised in the song of praise on the far shore of the Sea of Reeds, after the redemption from Egypt: 'In your [*chesed*] you will lead the people you have redeemed' (Exodus 15:13). God has said, 'I have seen . . . I have heard . . . I am concerned . . . I have come down to rescue them . . . and to bring them up' (Exodus 3:7–10). It is his *chesed* that causes God to respond in this way to his people's suffering, and it is on the basis of his *chesed* that they would, ever afterwards, call upon him for deliverance in trouble. So David's prayer was, 'Turn, O Lord, and deliver me; save me because of your [*chesed*] (Psalm 6:4).

Chesed is seen as being especially shown to Israel. Chief Rabbi Hertz[8], quoting from *The Prayer Book*[9], pointed out that this places upon the people a responsibility: 'With everlasting love Thou hast loved the House of Israel, Thy people; a Law and commandments, statutes and judgments hast Thou taught us. Therefore, O Lord our God, when we lie down and when we rise up we will meditate on Thy statutes; yea, we will rejoice in the words of Thy Law and in Thy commandments for ever; for they are our life and the strength of our days.'[10] The demands made by a holy God upon his people are a manifestation, not of tyranny, but of his *chesed* toward them.

Chesed is undeserved

Chesed is completely unmerited–it is the gift of God's grace (*chen*). Ezra recognised this as he offered praise to the Lord, who had 'extended his good favour [*chesed*] to me' (Ezra 7:28). Ezra knew that he was successful only because God's hand was with him, and God's hand was with him only because of his *chesed*. The Rabbis have said that 'beyond all human merit and deed are his compassion and His grace'.[11] Nowhere is this more true than in the area of forgiveness. 'Have mercy on me, O God, according to your *chesed*; according to your great compassion blot out my transgressions' prayed David after his sin with Bathsheba was exposed (Psalm 51:1). Forgiveness for sin can never, by its very nature, be deserved; it can only be claimed on the basis of God's *chesed*. But it *can* be claimed confidently, because this is the nature of God. And not to claim it is to deny his character.

Solomon ibn Gabirol,[12] medieval 'sweet singer of Israel', expressed the wonder of the grace which activates God's *chesed* to us:

I am unworthy of the saving grace
Thou hast to me Thy servant ever shown,
So must I waft my song of praise above,
And unto Thee my gratitude make known.[13]

Chesed with comfort and security

The writer of Psalm 119 yearned for spiritual comfort–for
God's compassion to be demonstrated in his personal
experience. He knew that, on his own part, this required
a faithfulness to and a delight in God's word. But it was
also dependent on God's grace: 'May your [*chesed*] be my
comfort,' he prayed (Psalm 119:76). David, on the other
hand, offered praise to God in a time of rejoicing,
acknowledging that his triumphs and blessings came
only from God–and his confidence for the future, likewise,
was in no way based upon his own strength: 'Surely you
have granted him eternal blessings . . . the king trusts in
the Lord; through the [*chesed*] of the Most High he will
not be shaken' (Psalm 21:6–7).

Chesed with love and mercy

Chesed is often linked with other qualities, and this
expands the revelation of God's character. Jeremiah
coupled God's chesed with his love: 'I have loved you,'
says the Lord to Israel, 'with an everlasting love; I have
drawn you with [*chesed*]' (Jeremiah 31:3). God has a relationship of love with this people, and that gives them a
special claim upon his *chesed*. In an altogether different
vein the prophet linked *chesed* with pity–mercy–as he
painted the picture of God's withdrawal of blessing from
a rebellious people: 'I have withdrawn my blessing, my
[*chesed*] and my pity [*rachamim*–'tender mercies'] from

this people' (Jeremiah 16:5). But God had not utterly deserted his people, acknowledged the writer of Lamentations: 'Because of the Lord's [great mercies] we are not consumed, for his compassions never fail. They are new every morning; great is your faithfulness' (Lamentations 3:22–23).

The Chassidic movement[14] came into being because there were those who yearned 'for communion with the Universal God, the Omnipresent Being Whose chief attributes in their eyes were Love, Forgiveness and Grace'.[15] The very name 'Chassidim' implies 'those who love God'.

Chesed with righteousness and justice

There is another, less palatable side to God's *chesed* shown us again through Jeremiah, as he challenged the people of his day to recognise 'the Lord, who exercises kindness [*chesed*], justice and righteousness' (Jeremiah 9:24). *Chesed* is not soft, malleable, tolerant. It wants the best for us and it expects the best of us. Anything less would not be truly loving or truly just. That is the nature of God–love and pity are balanced by justice and righteousness. This total revelation of God's character comes out most clearly in his self-revelation to Moses on Sinai after the golden calf incident: 'The Lord, the Lord, the compassionate and gracious God, slow to anger, abounding in [*chesed*] and faithfulness ['truth'–AV] . . . maintaining love . . . forgiving wickedness . . . Yet he does not leave the guilty unpunished' (Exodus 34:6–7). There is a steadfastness, an adherence to truth, about God's character that makes it unthinkable for him to tolerate or ignore evil. This too is an aspect of his *chesed*. And this is recognised in Jewish tradition.

The *Kabbalah*[16] teaches that 'The Talmudic Haggadah knows above all two principal qualities of God: chesed and *din*, love and stern judgment . . . God's love and His mercy are regarded as one and the same'.[17] And truth comes into the equation, to strike a balance between these two seemingly contradictory aspects of God's character. We see 'the attributes of *chesed* (grace), *din* (stern judgment) . . . among which *emeth* (truth) has the function of maintaining an equilibrium'.[18] In our own day Magonet, again commenting on Psalm 145, has said that *chesed* is allied with truth, righteousness and goodness.[19]

Chesed is abundant

Everything about God is so 'big', so without limits and boundaries, and the Hebrew writers sometimes tried to bring this out as they spoke of his *chesed*. 'As high as the heavens are above the earth, so *great* is his [*chesed*] for those who fear him,' declared David the psalmist (Psalm 103:11); and this generosity of love is displayed in the extent to which he is prepared to forgive, even to remove sin altogether. There simply are no limits to his *chesed*. Joel, too, spoke of this when he appealed to the people to return in repentance to God 'for he is gracious and compassionate, slow to anger and *abounding* in [*chesed*]' (Joel 2:13).

Chesed is everlasting

God's *chesed* is not only great in measure and in quantity; it is unlimited in time–everlasting. King David, on the day that he danced before the Lord in rejoicing as the ark was returned, called upon his people to join him in praise: 'Give thanks to the Lord, for he is good; his [*chesed*] endures *for ever*' (1 Chronicles 16:34), and this chorus is echoed from time to time throughout Israel's history: by Solomon at the building of the Temple (2 Chronicles 5:13); again at the dedication of the Temple (2 Chronicles 7:3,6); at the foundation of the second Temple under Ezra (Ezra 3:11); and, of course, throughout Psalm 136.

Jeremiah foresaw a day when, after the desolation which was to come, the land would be restored and this song would be heard again (Jeremiah 33:11). And Isaiah told of God's promise that, though God may seem to hide his face for a time, that time is just a brief moment: '"I hid my face from you for a moment, but with *everlasting* [*chesed*] I will have compassion on you," says the Lord your Redeemer' (Isaiah 54:8). God's anger is never the last word, because however long it lasts, his *chesed* goes on longer! It is no wonder that this unfailing, abounding, never-ending love is described as *good* (Psalm 69:16) in the sense of 'kind' and 'generous-hearted'.

Chesed and covenant

Chesed has been particularly demonstrated in God's relationship with Israel, 'in the many good things he has done for the house of Israel, according to his compassion and many 'loving-kindnesses' (Psalm 63:7). It is the essential component in his covenant relationship with his people. As Kaiser says, 'All Israel's freedom was owed to the loyal love (*chesed*) Yahweh had for His people.'[20] Moses spoke of the 'covenant of [*chesed*]' (Deuteronomy 7:9) and appealed, on its basis, for total obedience to God's commands (v.11). Daniel used the same expression, 'covenant of *chesed*', but he cited it as the reason for repentance. How could God's people have been so faithless to the God who had been so utterly faithful, reliable and true? This is the heart of the message of Hosea, whose ministry was to demonstrate in his own life the wonder of God's great *chesed* for Israel, which is yet allied to righteousness, justice, faithfulness: 'I will bethroth you to me for ever; I will betroth you in righteousness and justice, in [*chesed*] and compassion. I will betroth you in faithfulness, and you will acknowledge the Lord' (Hosea 2:19). God's *chesed* is the entire foundation of Israel's covenant relationship with him.

'Chesed is the only word Hosea had to describe the riches of God's grace in the heart of God.'[21] It is because of *chesed* that he would again betroth Israel to him–'because he loved your father, therefore he chose their seed after them' (Deuteronomy 7:9,12). God's *chesed* for Israel means that he will never give them up and let his anger overcome his compassion (Hosea 11:8–9). He is not a man, fickle in his affections–his holiness demands steadfastness. When his people turn, repenting, he will be gracious and heal (Hosea 14:2–4).

Micah recalled the ancient promise of *chesed* made to Israel's forefathers (Micah 7:20)–these promises are Israel's anchor and hope for the future. Particular mention is made of David and his house concerning this covenant *chesed*, in terms which are surely Messianic: 'He shows unfailing [*chesed*] to his anointed, to David and his descendants for ever' (2 Samuel 22:51).

Israel's relationship with God is that of covenant–a covenant based upon *chesed*. It is because of his *chesed* that God chose Israel to be his medium for blessing to all the nations (Deuteronomy 7:8). Magonet, again on Psalm 145, talks about 'the covenant with God which is sealed with *chesed*, faithful loyalty and love'.[22] And on Psalm 23, which he calls 'the nightingale of the Psalms', he says of verse 6, 'It is the language of the covenant promises which enters here, God's "tov va-chesed", God's goodness and faithful love . . . it suggests the security that comes from an existence within the covenant with God, the only certainty for the Psalmist in an uncertain world.'[23]

To the Gentiles too

Israel is not alone in being the object of God's *chesed*. She is meant to be the medium for the Gentile nations also to be blessed. The story of Jonah clearly demonstrates this. 'The theology of Jonah revolves around the extension of the grace of God to gentiles.'[24] God had to remind Jonah that to them too the Lord is 'a gracious, and compassionate God, slow to anger and abounding in [*chesed*]' (Jonah 4:2).

Chesed and the people of God

God's people are called to show *chesed* (kindness, mercy) in their dealings with one another and with the vulnerable. 'I desire mercy [*chesed*], not sacrifice' is God's complaint (Hosea 6:6), having charged them in the strongest terms: 'There is no faithfulness, no [*chesed*], no acknowledgment of God in the land. There is only cursing, lying and murder, stealing and adultery' (Hosea 4:1,2). 'Sow for yourselves righteousness, reap the fruit of [*chesed*],' he appeals to them (Hosea 10:12); 'Return to your God; maintain *chesed* and justice.' Micah, too, compared the value of ritual correctness with true godliness: 'He has showed you, O man, what is good. And what does the Lord require of you? To act justly and to love [*chesed*] and to walk humbly with your God' (Micah 6:8).

This is the response expected from a people to whom *chesed* has been given in such measure. And as with God's *chesed*, the love and the mercy are combined with sterner qualities of righteousness, justice and judgement, so it is to be with his people. 'Love is the height of goodness. It cannot be reached unless we have learned thoroughly the lessons of justice and righteousness. Where there is no justice and righteousness, there can be no love.'[25]

There is a word derived from *chesed*, and that is *chassid*. A chassid is a man who loves God and is devoted to him (Isaiah 57:1). Such a man is described as 'godly' or 'pious': 'The Lord has set apart the [*chassid*] for himself' (Psalm 4:3), and 'let everyone who is [*chassid*] pray to you' (Psalm 32:6). David once complained to God that the chassidim and the faithful had vanished, and there was only corruption and oppression (Psalm 12:1). The AV sometimes translated this word as 'holy', the NIV as 'devoted', as in 'Guard my life, for I am [*chassid*]' (Psalm 86:2). This 'devotion', a covenant word, describes a relationship like that between God and Israel, David and Jonathan (1 Samuel 20:14; 2 Samuel 9:3), husband and wife.

The Chassidim

The religious party of Maccabean times were known as 'Hasidaeans'–the 'pious ones'. They were the driving force in the struggle for independence. It was, after all, the priest Mattathias and his sons who, by their refusal to practise idolatry, sparked off the rebellion. But in medieval times an altogether new movement arose in Eastern Europe. A Rabbi known as the 'Baal Shem Tov'[26] began to teach his followers that true religion was not just a matter of Talmudic scholarship, but required also the element of love–love of God combined with warmth of faith and fervent prayer. This is the essence of Chassidism–to stress the subjective elements of feelings in faith, rather than the more objective dogma and ritual. 'A plain man,' taught the Baal Shem Tov, 'filled with a sincere belief in God, and whose prayers come from the heart, is more acceptable to God than the Rabbi versed in the Law, and who throughout his life is absorbed in the study of the Talmud and in the observance of petty ceremonials.'

And so Chassidism, that word derived from *chesed*, came to embrace the idea of communion between humankind and Almighty God. The Chassidim were men devoted to the worship and service of God. Chassidic Rabbis were, and still are today, seen to be invested with something of the aura of God's holiness and wisdom, even of his glory. That this deep, emotional love of God was to be extended to one's fellow men and women is shown by the story of a father who complained to the Besht that his son had forsaken God. What should he do about this son? After all, common practice was to disown the renegade. 'Love him more than ever' was the counsel he received.

A Chassid 'was simply one who practised chesed, whose heart and mind were suffused with a rich intensity of goodness . . . resulting in complete devotion to God and unqualified love of his fellow-men'.[27]

God so loved

In the New Testament Scriptures, God's love is supremely manifested in Jesus, particularly in his atoning death. Just as, for Israel, God's great revelation of *chesed* was his act of redemption from Egypt, so Jesus pointed forward to *his* redemptive work in the words, 'For God so loved the world that he gave his one and only Son, that whoever believes in him shall not perish but have eternal life' (John 3:16). Archbishop Temple[28] said of these words, 'This is the heart of the Gospel. Not "God is love"–a precious truth, but affirming no divine act for our redemption; "*God so loved that He gave*".[29] Here again is love in action–but what action, and at what cost!

God *is* love

God is not only the personification of love–he *is* love (1 John 4:8). This fact is proclaimed throughout the whole Bible–by his character as revealed in his actions. But here it is overtly stated: God is love. But, as in the Hebrew Scriptures, this does not mean that he is 'wet', a 'soft touch'. His character of love goes alongside, and is indeed enhanced by, his character of holiness–that righteousness and justice that we have already noted. Marshall puts it this way: 'God is all-loving and, equally, all-holy. These two characteristics do not stand in opposition to one another but belong together and determine His actions.'[30]

This character of love is revealed in God's readiness to forgive–that readiness which David the king claimed, which has been made freely available to everyone through the atoning blood of his Son, Jesus (1 John 1:7–9). As Marshall has said, 'Love means forgiving the sins of the beloved and remembering them no more. This is what God has done for rebellious mankind.'[31]

There are echoes of that 'great', 'everlasting', 'abundant' love proclaimed by the ancient prophets. John spoke in his Gospel of the full *extent* of the love of Jesus for 'his own': 'He loved them to the last'–or–'He now showed them the full extent of his love' (John 13:1). In his first letter, John tries to express the limitless, generous *quantity* of this love: 'How great is the love the Father has *lavished* on us' (1 John 3:1, my italics). There is simply no limit, in time or content, to God's love for us.

This is love

We have a definition of love in the New Testament Scriptures which puts into words what is implicit in the ancient, God-given, sacrificial system. 'This is how we know what love is: [Messiah] Jesus laid down his life for us' (1 John 3:16). This recalls the words of Jesus himself, recorded by John in his Gospel: 'Greater love has no-one than this, that he lay down his life for his friends' (John 15:13). *Chesed* is love expressed in action–here it is expressed in the most costly action. Jesus had described himself as 'the good shepherd', saying that such a shepherd lays down his life for the sheep (John 10:11). One is reminded again of the 'shepherd psalm', the 'Nightingale of Psalms', with its message of God's goodness and *chesed*.

Our response

It is not surprising that John, so absorbed by the wonder of God's great love, should be the one to issue the challenge of response, recalling the message of Hosea. 'Acceptance of the truth involves active love,' declares Marshall.[32] Love may not be expressed only in words–deeds are also necessary. What kind of love is it that does not produce love of one another? What kind of faith is it? 'John insists that Christian faith must issue in brotherly love, and the absence of love is proof of the absence of faith.'[33]

'The Biblical concept of love is distinctive, inasfar as it is associated with a God who enters into a covenant relationship with his people and maintains it with undeserved "steadfast love" (Deuteronomy 7:9). God's essential activity is saving love . . . and in the New Testament we find this activity centred in the person and work of

Jesus.'[34] It is the responsibility of the followers of Jesus to reflect his *chesed* in our own characters, actions and relationships.

Notes

1 Brown, Driver and Briggs.
2 Eric Lipson. Unpublished.
3 Montefiore and Loewe, *A Rabbinic Anthology* (Macmillan & Co., 1938), p.89.
4 Eric Lipson. Unpublished.
5 Samson Raphael Hirsch, *Horeb*, 1837 (Soncino Press, fourth edition, 1981), p.53.
6 Rabbi Jonathan Magonet, *A Rabbi Reads the Psalms* (SCM Press, 1994), p.42.
7 Eric Lipson. Unpublished.
8 Dr J.H. Hertz. Chief Rabbi of Great Britain in the early years of this century.
9 Singer, *The Authorised Jewish Prayer Book* (Eyre and Spottiswoode Ltd, 1957).
10 Dr J.H. Hertz, *A Book of Jewish Thoughts* (Oxford University Press 1920), p.212.
11 Montefiore and Loewe, *op. cit.*, p.89.
12 Solomon Ibn Gabirol. Spanish poet, philosopher, moralist. c.1021–1058.
13 *The Royal Crown.*
14 The eighteenth-century sect which sought to escape the confines of dry, academic Judaism.
15 *The Hasidic Anthology* (Charles Scribner's Sons, 1934), Introduction, p. lxxviii.
16 *Kabbalah*–a form of Jewish mysticism which arose in the late Middle Ages.
17 Gershom Scholem, *Origins of the Kabbalah* (Jewish Pub. Soc. Princeton University Press, 1990), p.144.
18 *Ibid.*

19 Rabbi Jonathan Magonet, *A Rabbi Reads the Psalms* (SCM Press 1994), p. 42.

20 Walter C. Kaiser, jr, *Towards and Old Testament Theology* (Zondervan, 1978), p.104.

21 *Ibid*, p.199.

22 R Jonathan Magonet. *A Rabbi Reads the Psalms* (SCM Press 1994) p. 42.

23 *Ibid.*, pp.66–67.

24 Walter C. Keiser Jnr., op. cit p.200.

25 Rabbi Dr Isidore Epstein, *Step by Step in the Jewish Religion* (Soncino Press, 1958), p.47.

26 Israel B. Eliezer. Commonly known as 'Besht'. c.1700–1760. Founder of Chassidism.

27 Rabbi Dr Louis Jacobs, *Hasidic Prayer* (Schocken Books: New York, third printing, 1975), p.2.

28 William Temple. Archbishop of Canterbury in the middle years of the twentieth century.

29 William Temple, *Readings in St John's Gospel* (Macmillan, 1945).

30 *New International Commentary on The Epistles of John* (Eerdmans, 1978), p.213.

31 *Ibid.*, p.215.

32 *Ibid.*, p.62.

33 *Ibid.*, p.54.

34 Stephen S. Smalley, *Word Biblical Commentary, 1,2,3 John* (Word), p.61.

תּוֹרָה

She put the phone down; she was shaking. Life had been stressful these past few months. A bereavement in the middle of moving house; and now–out of the blue–a most devastating phone call, late at night, totally unexpected. What was going on? Had they, after all these years of walking with the Lord, got their guidance wrong? 'What do we do?' 'Which way do we turn?' Panic.

'Come on,' he said. 'Let's get the Bible out and see what God has to say.'

'Submit to God and be at peace with Him . . . If you . . . assign your nuggets to the dust, your gold . . . to the rocks in the ravines, then the Almighty will be your gold, the choicest silver for you. Surely then . . . you will pray to Him, and He will hear you . . . What you decide on will be done, and light will shine on your ways' (Job 22:21–28).

That was the word they needed to hear just then. It set their priorities in perspective. It restored peace, and confidence in God. The situation was unchanged, but direction and light had been reintroduced.

'Great peace have they who love your [*Torah*]' (Psalm 119:165).

5

TORAH

תורה

'Blessed be the Lord, Who has chosen us out of all the peoples of the world with this everlasting trust, and gave us His *Torah*.'[1] These words express the sense of privilege that Israel has always felt at being chosen by God to be entrusted with *Torah*, not just for themselves, but for all peoples. Of all the gifts that God has showered upon Israel, *Torah* stands supreme. It is 'the holiest possession of Israel.'[2] It was a precious charge given to Moses on Sinai; Moses 'handed it down to Joshua; Joshua to the Elders; the Elders to the Prophets; and the Prophets handed it down to the men of the Great assembly.'[3]

The giving of *Torah* at Sinai is commemorated at the festival of Pentecost, when the following prayer is recited during Evening Service:

With everlasting love Thou hast loved the house of Israel, Thy people; a law and commandments, statutes and judgments hast Thou taught us. Therefore, O Lord our God, when we lie down and when we rise up, we will meditate on Thy statutes, and we will rejoice in the words of Thy Law and

in Thy commandments for ever and ever; for they are our life
and the length of our days, and on them we will meditate day
and night.

It is true that 'the *Torah* has preserved the Jew as the
Jew has preserved *Torah*'.[4]

What is *Torah*?

When the Rabbis use the word *Torah* it is not always easy
to know exactly what they mean. Historically the word
has been, and still is, used to convey different ideas. It can
mean: 1) The ten 'Words' (Commandments) of Exodus 20;
2) That part of Exodus which commences at chapter 12; 3)
The five books of Moses known as the Pentateuch (the
first five books of the Bible); 4) The Hebrew Scriptures
(Old Testament); 5) The whole written and oral law
traditionally handed to Moses on Sinai, which includes
the *Talmud*.

In the prayer quoted above we see a hint of the breadth
of the meaning of the word *Torah*. *Torah* is more than law.
'Law' is a legal concept, particularly in Greek culture,
upon which our society is largely founded. 'Law' in this
sense is just a part of *Torah*, which is multi-faceted. We
can see this by simply reading through Psalm 119. It is, for
example, 'way' (v.1), and 'light' (v.105). That implies
'direction' and 'revelation'. It is God's 'word' (v.89) of
grace to us, not–as with the Greek *nomos* (translated
'law')–standing in opposition to grace.

The word *Torah* is related to *yarah*–'to shoot at a
target'. This, according to the lexicon, is a causative
word, active; 'indicating, pointing, penetrating, shooting,
throwing, making changes, altering that which is touched
or has been hit by an arrow either gently or with violence.'

It is a travesty to describe *Torah* as 'law'–immutable,
unchanging, rigid. 'It is in truth our loving Father's
direction-finder for every person.'[5] More than that, it is
'both direction and route; the aim and the practice . . .
guide and teaching . . . God's "how" for mankind.'[6]

Torah is not so much a legal code as an ethical guide,
particularly for those in covenant relationship with the
Torah-giver. How do we recognise those in covenant relationship with Yahweh (the LORD)? Surely it is by whether
they do or do not do certain things–by the lives which they
live. And the standard for that living is *Torah*: 'Listen and
learn to fear the Lord your God and follow carefully all
the words of this [*Torah*]' (Deuteronomy 31:12). Probably
the best translation of the word *Torah* is 'teaching' or
'direction.' It is 'a fountain of life'.[7] It 'glows with the
life of revelation, law and promise'.[8] It is 'the communica-
tion of the very heart and mind of God'.[9]

The instrument of creation

Torah is eternal (Psalm 119:89). Talmudic tradition, based
on Proverbs 8:22, is that *Torah* was created before the
world: 'God created the Law before He created the world.'[10]
More than that; long before Jesus was born it was believed
that '*Torah* is a living creature . . . God held counsel with
Torah at the creation of the world';[11] that *Torah* was the
instrument of creation: 'Beloved are Israel, for unto them
was given the desirable instrument (*Torah*); but it was by a
special love that it was made known to them that that
desirable instrument was theirs, through which the world
was created.'[12] This belief is foundational: 'Simon the Just
. . . used to say, Upon three things the world is based:
upon the Torah, upon divine worship, and upon acts of
benevolence.'[13]

Torah Min Ha-Shamayim

Torah is seen as eternal, a living creative force which nestled at God's side before creation. But then, at Sinai, *Torah* was revealed–directly from heaven (*min ha-shamayim*)–to Israel by means of Moses; revealed as God's word/communication, God's teaching, God's direction. The revelation of *Torah* from heaven is the eighth principle of the Jewish faith. So it is altogether logical to say that 'Judaism stands or falls with its belief in the historic actuality of the Revelation at Sinai'.[14] To Jewish people *Torah* has always been 'the central organising principle of our religious ideas–the vital expression of our everlasting covenant with God'.[15] 'Torah is Israel's soul, Torah is Israel's life.'[16] *Torah* is even the purpose for which Israel was created: 'Unlike other nations, where the law is created for the nation, in Israel the nation was created for the Law.'[17]

The reading of Torah is central to Jewish public worship in the synagogue, following the tradition of Ezra, who assembled all the people and 'brought the [Torah] before the assembly . . . read it aloud from daybreak till noon . . . in the presence of the men, women and others who could understand' (Nehemiah 8:2–3). The five books of Moses are read through each year, Sabbath by Sabbath. The scrolls themselves are treated with the utmost reverence. They are kept in a cupboard–the 'ark'–at the east end of the synagogue, before which a lamp is kept perpetually burning, testimony that 'your word is a lamp to my feet' (Psalm 119:105) and that 'the lamp of the Lord searches the spirit of man' (Proverbs 20:27).

'The scroll's presence in the congregation has something of the significance of the Mace in Parliament. They are the symbol of Authority. The Sovereignty of God and of His

Word is supreme.'[18] On the final day of *Succoth* (the Festival of Tabernacles) the last section of Deuteronomy is read, followed immediately by the first section of Genesis, so that there is no break in the continuity. This day is known as *Simchat Torah* (the 'Rejoicing of the Law'). The five scrolls, dressed in ornate 'mantles', are paraded around the synagogue, and the atmosphere is highly festive. This is Israel, giving annual expression to her sense of privilege and joy in the possession of God's *Torah*. This day is the culmination of the festival–the third of the three great pilgrim festivals of the Jewish year (Leviticus 23; Deuteronomy 16).

A boy's religious coming-of-age (and often, nowadays, a girl's too) is marked by his being called up, on the first Sabbath after his thirteenth birthday, to read the set portion from *Torah*. Much preparation (and nervous tension) goes into this. The portions are several chapters in length; the Hebrew in the scrolls has no pointing for the vowels–all has to be learned; and the chant, too, must be memorised. As if all this were not sufficient of an ordeal, the lad is expected to give a short exposition on the portion at the celebratory lunch afterwards. There is an inescapable connection between 'maturity' and the ability to read, understand and interpret *Torah*. Only now can this young man take his place fully among the men of Israel.

It is portions of *Torah* which are contained in the *tefillin* (phylacteries)–small boxes which are bound upon the arm and the forehead for the recital of daily prayers in the home. And it is portions of *Torah* which are contained in the *mezuza*–seen placed obliquely on the door-post of every religious Jewish home. This is in literal obedience to Deuteronomy 6:8–9.

So we can see that *Torah* is much more than 'law', or words on stone or parchment, or even instructions. It is a concept bound up, from ancient times, with life, light, eternity, creation–the personality of God himself.

Not just for Israel

If *Torah* was involved in creation, it must be a force for producing order out of chaos; 'The all-encompassing intelligent will of God manifesting itself in the creation and preservation of the world' as well as 'an eternal and unerring guide and ruler of mankind'.[19] This wisdom, this morality, is concerned not only with Israel, but with all of life. Israel was entrusted with *Torah*, not for privilege or enjoyment, but to be a blessing to all the nations of the world. For *Torah* was not given to create bondage. On the contary, 'The entire purpose of the Torah was to purify and elevate human existence'.[20] 'Great is the Torah which gives life to those that practise it.'[21]

The Messianic age–a 'new' *Torah*?

At the time when Jesus stepped visibly into history, there was a firm belief in the immutability of *Torah*. It could never change. Yet even in this belief there was something of an ambivalence. The *Targum*[22] on Isaiah 12:3 says, 'Ye shall receive new instruction–from the Chosen of Righteousness.' Professor Daube's[23] interpretation of this comment is: 'Ye shall receive a new law from those chosen in righteousness–ie in the Messianic Age.' The *Midrash*[24] on Canticles 2:13 expressly states that Messiah would give Israel a new Law.

Leo Baeck[25] has written: 'In the first century the belief was widespread among the Jews that world history consisted of three epochs: first the period of chaos; then the period of the *Torah*, beginning with the Revelation on Mt

Sinai; and finally the hoped-for period of the Messiah . . .
When all is fulfilled, and the Messiah has come, the period
of the law will have come to its close.'[26]

Landman, commenting on Jeremiah 31:31, wrote:
'Jewish Law could only be realised in its totality in a world
ruled by the Messiah.'[27] And W.D. Davies said that in the
Talmudic era, 'Despite the doctrine of the immutability of
the Torah, there were also occasional expressions of expectation that Torah would suffer modification in the
Messianic Age'.[28]

These beliefs, and this ambivalence, were the context in
which Jesus stepped visibly into history.

Jesus' attitude to *Torah*

Matthew 5:17–20 summarises Jesus' attitude to *Torah*.
There are four points worth noting in this passage: 1)
Jesus saw himself as coming, not to abolish *Torah*, but
to fulfil (or complete) it (v.17); 2) Jesus taught that
Torah would remain unchanged 'until everything is
accomplished'. He did not clarify the meaning of those
words (v.18); 3) Jesus' disciples should know that
practising and *teaching Torah* is what matters in the
kingdom of heaven (v.19). This is surely a reference to
those who value above all else the study alone of *Torah*
for its own sake; 4) Jesus, far from lowering the
standard of *Torah*, taught that *more* righteousness than
that of the Pharisees and scribes is required for entry
into the kingdom (v.20).

The last two of those points are purely practical. What
place should *Torah* have in the lives of Jesus' disciples? Is
it purely for ourselves or is it to share? Is its study to
increase our head knowledge or is it to change our lives?
Did Jesus come to make it easier–or harder–to gain

acceptance with God? Or was he saying that the written *Torah* was not the way to achieve that acceptance?

The first two points are more mystical. In what way (or ways) would Jesus fulfil–or complete–*Torah*? How was he interpreting the word *Torah* at that moment? And what did he mean by the expression 'until everything is accomplished'? Was it 'the end of the world'? Was it 'when all *Torah's* requirements have been met'? Was it 'when all that *Torah* looks to has arrived'? Could that 'fulfilment' mean 'the coming of Messiah'? Was he saying that when that happens, some of *Torah's* regulations will have fulfilled their role and become no longer applicable? This is the interpretation commonly given by Christian teachers, but perhaps it is one which needs a fresh appraisal. The passage raises a host of questions, and deserves more than a slick, simplistic and–dare I say it?–arrogant interpretation.

In Mark 7, Jesus' approach is presented differently. It seems that he was judging the Pharisees for demanding *more*, of *more people*, than *Torah* originally did. He was attacking the 'fence' which the Rabbis had erected around *Torah*. Rabbi Akiba said, 'Tradition is a fence for *Torah*.'[29] The original purpose of this fence was admirable in its way; it was to give a safety margin, so to speak; an extra protection against the possibility of infringement. 'Those to whom it was committed made a fence for its protection . . . that its sacred meaning should be handed down from age to age unimpaired and unchanged.'[30] But it had certainly become an 'adding to' God's original 'word'. Is it possible that Christians also have been guilty of this during the past two thousand years? The *protection* of *Torah* had degenerated into a *tampering* with *Torah*.

As in the Matthew passage, Mark shows Jesus as not lowering the expected standard–not lightening the demands for purity. Rather he was lifting those demands onto an altogether higher plane, focusing on the need for that inner cleansing and renewal of heart envisaged by Jeremiah (chapter 31) and Ezekiel (chapter 36). Certainly his summary of the law (Mark 12:28–31) was an affirmation of written *Torah* (Deuteronomy 6:4–6 and Leviticus 19:18).

It does seem that, not only in his teaching but also in his practice, Jesus had a revolutionary attitude to the various aspects of *Torah*. Moral requirements seemingly weighed more with him than ceremonial ones. Although he perhaps avoided confrontations concerning the latter, he certainly did not concerning the former. And he was scathing about laws which were purely traditional, while giving unfailing respect to biblical *Torah*. This has caused confusion among evangelical Christians throughout history–and continues to do so, particularly for Messianic Jews, who are concerned to give meaning to their Jewish identity and recover some of what has been lost in the predominantly Gentile Christian Church at large, while remaining true to their Messiah, Jesus. Our Messianic brothers and sisters value, where they find it, our understanding of their search for biblical, *Torah*-true, integrity.

Edersheim,[31] interestingly, argued that Jesus' whole stance towards *Torah* was different from the customary Rabbinic one. He contrasted the optimistic, upbeat, tone of 'The poor in spirit . . . theirs is the kingdom of heaven' (Matthew 5:3) with the much more pessimistic 'Ever be more and more lowly in spirit, since the expectancy of man is to become the food of worms'.[32] And Jesus' attitude was so positive; compare 'So in everything, do to others what you would have them do to you, for this sums up the Law and the Prophets' (Matthew 7:12) with

'What is hateful to thee, do not to another. That is the whole Law; all else is only explanation'.[33]

It is not only Christians who see this difference. Klausner noted that although very little of Jesus' ethical teaching was new, there was a difference in that it was not lost in a sea of legal prescription. This, to him, was what was revolutionary about Jesus' teaching: 'A man like Jesus, for whom the ethical ideal was everything, was something hitherto unheard-of in the Judaism of the day.'[34] To Klausner this was unacceptable and unworkable–the one cannot survive without the other, which he saw as the essential expression of identity. Jesus' attitude was altogether different; he emphasised underlying principles rather than details of practice; attitudes and relationships took precedence in his scale of values. And raised like a banner over the collected tradition of centuries came the startling challenge: 'The work of God is this: to believe in the one he has sent' (John 6:29). Surely Jesus had come full circle back to the opening statement of the Decalogue: 'I AM the LORD your God' (Exodus 20:1). The basis of *Torah* is the personality of God.

Perhaps what is most significant about Jesus' attitude to *Torah* is not so much the difference of emphasis as the constant repetition of the words, 'But I tell you . . . .' These words have to prompt the question, 'Who is this man?' Surely the primary impact of the sermon on the mount is not that it is a new understanding of the Law, but that it points to the identity and significance of Jesus himself.

Torah and *Logos*

The prologue to John's Gospel tells us that John recognised the importance of this question, and was answering it in a way that was intelligible to the largest possible number of his contemporaries. 'In the beginning was the [*Logos*]' (John 1:1), *Logos* was a Greek (Stoic) concept of the 'principle of reality'. Philo[35] adapted this idea, teaching that the *Logos* was the means by which men and women might know God. From here it was a short step to identify *Logos* with *Torah*. So Jeremias tells us that 'In the world of Hellenistic Judaism . . . the 'Word' was spoken of as the revelation of God . . . the concept of the personified Logos as the means of God's revelation.'[36] And John identified that *Logos*–that *Torah*–with Jesus.

Archbishop Temple[37] explained that *Logos* combines two meanings: 1) The Word of the Lord by which the heavens were made, and which came to the prophets; 2) The Rational Principle which gives unity and significance to all existing things.

> Philo himself had effected the combination of the Old Testament 'Word' with the Stoic 'Logos' . . . John is here following the thought of Philo . . . seeking common ground with his readers. So–the Jew will remember that 'By the Word of the Lord were the heavens made' and will think of '*Torah*'. The Greek will think of the 'Rational Principle'. Both will agree that this 'Logos' is the starting point of all things. It exists as it always did–in the beginning, at the root of the universe. The subject for which John is claiming their attention is the ultimate and supreme principle of the universe.[38]

This is that mighty and creative 'Word of the Lord'–*Torah*– there before creation; even God's instrument of creation; embodying life, light, eternity; God in self-revelation. 'Anyone who has seen me has seen the Father' (John 14:9).

The writer to the Hebrews used the same entrée to his readers' minds: '[God] . . . has spoken to us by his Son . . . through whom he made the universe' (Hebrews 1:2).

When *Torah* came at Sinai the glory of the Lord settled on the mountain. When Jesus walked this earth, John could say, 'We have seen his glory . . . full of grace and truth' (John 1:14). Jesus was 'the radiance of God's glory' (Hebrews 1:3). Temple summed it all up with the words: 'He Who tabernacled among men under the name of Jesus is the eternal Word of God, Himself God, the Agent of creation.' He was the *Logos*, God's instrument of creation.

Jesus was a master of the indirect claim. Often it is only with the knowledge of certain Rabbinic traditions that one can discern what he was actually saying. So it is, surely, with these words: 'Take my yoke upon you and learn from me' (Matthew 11:29). One of the ancient descriptions of *Torah* was that of a 'yoke': 'Whoso receives upon himself the yoke of Torah, from him the yoke of the kingdom and the yoke of worldly care will be removed.'[39] Here is another saying: 'Whoever dishonours the *Torah* will himself be dishonoured by mankind.'[40] Surely Jesus had this in mind when he said, 'Whoever acknowledges me before men, I will also acknowledge him before my Father in heaven. But whoever disowns me before men, I will disown him before my Father in heaven' (Matthew 10:32–33). Jesus knew he was himself God's *Torah*.

Law and grace

Torah is not legal–it is directional. Jesus, God's *Torah*, came not to restrict and imprison but to liberate and to demonstrate: 'If the Son sets you free, you will be free indeed' (John 8:36). The error that Paul was seeking to correct in his 'law and grace' diatribes was not that of believing, honouring and following *Torah*. It was the equating of *Torah* with *nomos* and with the traditions of the fathers. The early believers needed to shake off the shackles of their past conditioning; the Gentiles of their linguistic understanding of the word 'law'; the Jews of the historic 'fence' which Rabbinic tradition had set around *Torah*.

True *Torah*, truly understood, is the written expression of the personality of God. The same personality which has been revealed in the man Jesus–'the exact representation of his being' (Hebrews 1:3); 'full of grace and truth' (John 1:14). *Torah* was given as an expression of the character of God–his holiness and righteousness, yes–but also his *chesed*: his faithful, merciful, love.

Torah and Jesus

Who is this man? 'Where did he get his wisdom?' (Matthew 13:54). Here is the conclusion arrived at by a notable Messianic Jew of this century

> Sinai was where a people's training for their future work (to bless and bring blessing to the families of the earth) took place . . . Moses, the foundation, compiled the five books of *Torah*, and Jesus was the structure, the exegesis. Jesus the incarnate Word–Who was and continued to be God's instrument of creation–was the only One entitled to teach *Torah* and its meaning to mankind. He was the demonstration of how to live–and love. Jesus . . . was from the beginning the Father's instrument of creation and was *Torah* incarnate.[41]

Notes

1 Ber.1:4.
2 Samson Raphael Hirsch, *Horeb*, 1837 fourth edition (Soncino Press, fourth edition, 1981), para. 700.
3 Avoth 1:1.
4 Eric Lipson. Unpublished.

5 *Ibid.*

6 *Ibid.*

7 Dr J.H. Hertz *A Book of Jewish Thoughts*, (Oxford University Press, 1920), p. 214.

8 Dr Harold Reinhart (Minister, Westminster Synagogue), *Sifre Torah* (CCJ, 1964).

9 Eric Lipson. Unpublished.

10 H. Polano, *The Talmud* (Fredrick Warne and Co.) p.245.

11 *The Jewish Encyclopedia* (Funk and Wagnalls Co., 1903).

12 Avoth 3:18.

13 Avoth 1:2.

14 Dr J.H Hertz, *Commentary on Exodus* (Oxford University Press, 1930), p.234.

15 Dr Normon Solomon, *Jewish Chronicle*, 9 February 1996.

16 Samson Raphael Hirsch, *op. cit.*, para. 599.

17 *Ibid.*, para. 714.

18 Eric Lipson, *Approaching the Jew* (Wickliffe Press, 1966), p.11.

19 Eric Lipson. Unpublished.

20 Rabbi Dr A. Cohen, *Everyman's Talmud* (J.M. Dent and Sons Ltd., 1937), p.160.

21 Avoth 6:17.

22 Aramaic translation of the Hebrew Scriptures.

23 Twentieth-century Jewish philosopher.

24 Talmudic commentary.

25 Twentieth-century Reform Rabbi.

26 *The Pharisees.*

27 Leo Landman, *Messianism in the Talmudic Era* (KTAV Publishing House Inc., 1979), p.xxv.

28 W.D. Davies, *Ibid.*, p.243.

29 Avoth 3:17.

30 Avoth 3:17.

31 Hebrew Christian theologian of the late nineteenth century.

32 *Life and Times of the Messiah* (Longmans, Green and Co., seventh edition, 1892), pp.531–532.

33 Shab.31a.

34 Dr Joseph Klausner, *Jesus of Nazareth* (George Allen and Unwin Ltd, 1925), pp.385–389.

35 Jewish Alexandrian philosopher, about the time of Jesus.

36 Joachim Jeremias, *The Central Message of the New Testament* (SCM, 1965), p.87.

37 Late Archbishop of Canterbury.

38 *Readings in St John's Gospel* (Macmillan and Co., Ltd., 1945), chapter 1.

39 Avoth 3:6.

40 Avoth 4:8.

41 Eric Lipson. Unpublished.

A young Jewish minister stood in his synagogue in front of the ark (the cupboard in which the scrolls of Scripture are housed). Steeped in the ways of his people, he was troubled concerning another 'way' that he could not get out of his mind; the 'way' of one who had claimed to be his people's Messiah, but whose followers he had been taught, by precept and by experience, to regard as the enemies of his people. The history of 'Christian' anti-semitism, the teaching of his parents, the memory of taunts and bullying in his school-days; how could this possibly be truth?

Even if Jesus *were* the Messiah, how could he–the first-born son and grandson of Jewish ministers, the focus of all their hopes–do this to his family; cut himself off from his people! It was impossible. He came to a decision. 'If truth lies that way, I can't follow it.'

God was saying, 'This is the way, walk ye in it.' But the price was too high–not just for himself, but for his loved ones. The time was not yet ripe for him to become a follower, to walk in the way of Yeshua ben David, Messiah of Israel.

6

HALACHAH

הלכה

Halachah. The word is derived from the verb 'to go', 'to walk', and has developed to embrace the idea of 'way of life'. Psalm 15:2 expresses this as it extols the one whose 'walk' is upright, blameless. The prophet Nathan used the same root word in his parable to David, after the seduction of Bathsheba and the murder of Uriah: 'Now a "traveller" came to a rich man,' he begins his story (2 Samuel 12:2); a 'traveller'–one who 'walks' a path, a way. So *Halachah* has come to mean, primarily, the way in which one should walk, 'the way in which a Jew should conduct himself.'[1] Dr Cohen[2] said, 'Halachah denotes "walking", and indicates the way of life to tread in conformity with the precepts of Torah.'[3] It is also understood as a 'way of acting, habit, usage . . . custom and the norm of practice'.[4]

Halachah, said Rabbi Jacobs, 'is the legal side of Judaism, the legal discussions of the Rabbis.' Technically, *Halachah* is comprised of *Mishnah*, and the section of *Gemara* which deals with law–legal matters. Traditionally, as Dr Cohen put it in *Everyman's Talmud*, it is 'the logical

95

working out by many generations of devoted scholars of the theory devised by Ezra for the salvation of the people of Israel'. *Halachah* is the altogether distinctive code of Jewish conduct, and has been largely responsible for keeping alive the Jewish consciousness. 'The law of Moses cannot be altered, but interpretation of it may give the appearance of its having been changed and certainly considerably augmented . . . case law can be as binding as an original enactment'.[5]

The Hebrew Scriptures

In the fortieth year of their wanderings, Moses called the people of Israel together to reiterate what God had told them at Sinai. He enjoined them not to turn aside from the path God had commanded them to walk in. 'Walk in all the way that the Lord your God has commanded you' (Deuteronomy 5:33) was his call as he neared the end of his life. He may perhaps have been recalling the wise counsel given to him by his father-in-law so many years before: 'Show them the way to live' (literally, 'The way wherein they should walk') (Exodus 18:20).

This is the legacy Moses wanted to leave behind–not so much the memory of *his* exploits as the present and on-going reality of a people 'walking' in all the way that the Lord had commanded them. He came back to this theme later, when warning them of the dangers of idolatry and of false prophets and miracle-workers: 'It is the Lord your God you must follow' (literally, 'Walk after the Lord your God') (Deuteronomy 13:4). And in the interests of justice, mercy and the prevention of innocent blood-shed, he brought love into the equation: 'Love the Lord your God and . . . walk always in his ways' (Deuteronomy 19:9). Surely the implication is that as God is himself a

God of love, so to walk in his ways will be to walk in a loving manner to one another.

Many failures later, God is portrayed as crying out to his people in their distress and fear: 'If my people would but listen to me, If Israel would follow [walk in] my ways' (Psalm 81:13). And the call is to individuals as well as to the nation. David came to realise that the way out of his difficulties was not to find a solution of man's devising. He may have begun his plea, 'Hear my prayer, listen to my cry . . . come to my relief,' but he knew he must come to the point of submission with, 'Show me the way I should go' (Psalm 143:8).

Isaiah, sent to recall the people to righteousness when inevitable disaster loomed, called, invitingly, 'Come, O house of Jacob, let us walk in the light of the Lord' (Isaiah 2:5). And he spoke of a time to come when, although the Lord would have given them 'the bread of adversity and the water of affliction', there would be a return to God; they would once again hear and heed God's voice, saying, 'This is the way; walk in it' (Isaiah 30:20–21).

Micah had encapsulated the ideal of *Halachah* in his core teaching, 'He has showed you, O man, what is good. And what does the Lord require of you? To act justly and to love mercy and to walk humbly with your God' (Micah 6:8). And this 'walk' with the Lord, in his ways, became the ideal of righteousness, so that historical figures were defined by their 'walk'. What better eulogy to the memory of King Josiah than to say, simply, that 'he . . . walked in the ways of his father David, not turning aside to the right or to the left' (2 Chronicles 34:2). And what more damning epitaph on King Zimri than 'he died, because of the sins he had committed, doing evil in the eyes of the Lord and walking in the ways of Jeroboam' (1 Kings 16:19).

Many times, the Scriptures tell us, God warned his people not to go after their own ways but his. There was even an incident recorded in Jeremiah, when the leaders asked the prophet to pray that God would show them the way to go. The prophet did so, and they promised to abide by whatever God said. But when the answer came, it was rejected. 'You are lying,' they said to Jeremiah. The way commanded by God was unacceptable to them, and as a result they went into exile (Jeremiah 42 and 43). But there was light beyond the darkness. In the time to come, wrote Micah, 'many nations–not Israel alone–would stream to the House of the Lord, saying, 'Come, let us go up to the mountain of the Lord . . . He will teach us his ways, so that we may walk in his paths' (Micah 4:2).

Rabbinic tradition

The term *Halachah* is used to describe the oral tradition concerning 'interpretations, discussions and controversies connected with the *legal* part of the Scriptures',[6] as opposed to *Haggadah*, which deals with narrative. It is, in fact, the body of traditional, religious law, worked out during the centuries, as conditions changed. 'The law was interpreted for each generation, in the light of its particular problems, according to certain legal principles on the basis of God's Word and in accordance with common sense and agreed local customs.'[7] 'Eventually, after much debate, the codes of the great Rabbis Maimonides[8] and Joseph Caro[9] became generally accepted as authoritative.'[10] Maimonides' approach was more rationalistic, Caro's more that of a mystic. Caro's *Shulchan Aruch* ('Set Table', 'Code') has been immensely influential in Judaism–a force recognised by both Eastern and Western Jews.

Friedlander[11] classified *Halachah* into different groups in this way:

1) That which is directly or indirectly derived from the Pentateuch.
2) That which traces its origin to Moses or the remote past.
3) That which originated between the Pentateuch and the close of the Hebrew Scriptures.
4) That which was introduced post-biblically.
5) That which has no authority or text, but simply long usage.[12]

We can see that this covers a wide range! The body of *Halachah* is indeed vast. There are 'the interpretations of the Pentateuchal law, the enormous elaborations of it, the immense additions to it, the interminable discussions, arguments, disputations and counter-arguments; all this is Halachah'.[13]

Halachah covers the whole way of life of the Jew–how he should conduct himself in any and all circumstances; 'the rules and patterns of Jewish behaviour'.[14] It is the legal side of Judaism. When there is doubt about a matter, one asks, 'What is the *Halachah* here?' It is the 'final decision of legal matters'.[15] 'It determined the nature of the Jew's life in exile, the only frame in which a life in the light of Sinaitic revelation seemed possible.'[16]

These traditions are authoritative for the Jew; as authoritative as Scripture itself. Sometimes, in fact, the word *Torah* is used to include this oral tradition–about which it is said, 'Moses received Torah from Sinai and delivered it to Joshua, and Joshua to the Elders, and the Elders to the Prophets, and the Prophets delivered it to the Men of the Great Synagogue.'[17] 'The chain of tradition then passed through the High Priest Simon the Just (third

century BC), Antigonos of Socho and so through a
succession of learned leaders to Hillel and Shammai,
who were old when Jesus was a lad.'[18] These said three
things: 'Be deliberate in judging, and raise up many
disciples, and make a hedge for the Torah.'[19]

'The Jew is enjoined to walk in traditional practice and
custom, the adopted opinions of ancient sages whose final
views, arrived at on such data as they had before them and
had the capacity to understand. Ever after they are
accepted as immutable.'[20] Dr Cohen, in the introduction
to his translation of *Berachot*,[21] said that Rabbinic Judaism
aimed at controlling the whole life of its adherents. Nothing could be outside its purview. The theory upon which
this is based is scriptural. 'What is a brief passage,' asks a
Rabbi, 'upon which all the principles of the *Torah*
depend?' 'In all thy ways acknowledge him, and he will
direct thy paths' (Proverbs 3:6). Guidance is offered for
every conceivable experience of life.

The very comprehensiveness of this view has meant, of
course, that *Halachah* has had to develop progressively in
order to handle new situations and circumstances which
the ancients could never have envisaged. In his introduction to *Everyman's Talmud*, Dr Cohen said, 'They [the
Pharisees and the Rabbis] made it a means of ethical
training by defining right conduct in terms of a progressive morality.'

Chief Rabbi Sacks[22] has said that *Halachah* includes
two things: 'A process or a product, the process of study-
ing Jewish law or the product of that study, the law
itself.'[23] That is why study is so important; it is an essential
part of the 'walk'. As the Rabbis study, they come to
conclusions, and their conclusions are authoritative.
That is how one discerns how to walk in the ways of
God. 'A Halachic decision is a practical definition of the

way a person must actually behave in any situation.'[24] Judaism is essentially a practical religion; what matters is what one *does*–how one behaves. Are my *actions* right? And so Chief Rabbi Sacks quotes Rabbi J.B. Soloveitchik[25] thus: 'Halachah–the visible surface of a philosophy: the only philosophy that could lay legitimate claim to being Jewish.'[26]

Over the years

Halachah developed over the centuries as oral tradition. This practice itself, however, became hardened into dogma, as there grew up a belief that to write it down was almost an act of sacrilege 'tantamount to burning the Torah'.[27] The reasoning was that 'reduction to writing tends to deaden';[28] that, with the loss of fluidity and flexibility, can come the loss of life. This attitude eventually gave way 'as Rome tightened its grip on Judaea and the danger became apparent that those who carried traditions in their memories might not survive'.[29] The Rabbis–and there were very many–gave themselves totally to the development of *Halachah*, 'which could be established by Scriptural proof, tradition or custom, earlier Rabbinic authority or by majority decision'.[30]

The best minds of a gifted people were spent in the ordering of what was to be the accepted way of life. The discussions were not always peaceful nor the conclusions unanimous. Sometimes, in fact, there have been contradictory decisions; views differed about which source was the authoritative one, and which method should be followed. So one finds the wording, 'Rabbi X said . . . , but Rabbi Y said'. . . . 'On the other hand' is a very Jewish expression! *Halachah* was eventually written down and codified as part of the Talmud. It still exercises and trains the minds of religious Jews. But it is not only an intellectual exercise.

Halachah has been crucial to the history of the Jewish people since ancient times in two ways. It has kept the Jew true religiously, dictating his way of life in such a way as to make it difficult for him not to conform; it 'moulded the existence of the Jew ... directed his steps so that he walked humbly with his God'.[31] And it was the firm ground under his feet in what has more often than not been a bewildering, insecure and unpredictable environment: 'It created a breakwater, behind which he found security from the alien influences that tended to sweep him from his racial moorings.'[32]

A dead system?

Halachah looks to the uninitiated–even to many Jews–like a mass of legality, tying its adherents up into paralysis. The accusation has been made that the whole system is 'an intolerable incubus'.[33] In latter years, Rabbis have sought to give the lie to the belief widely held in modern times that it is 'a system of dry legalism devoid of all spiritual content'.[34] Certainly it seems at times to deal only with externals and minutiae but, it is claimed, there is life lying under the surface. 'The refreshing springs of religion were not blocked as a consequence.'[35] In modern times Rabbi Louis Jacobs has declared that *Halachic* deeds are undergirded with 'beliefs that provide the deed with its sanction and infuse it with life'.[36]

The modern dilemma

Rabbi Jacobs' writings have represented a determined effort to present Judaism as a viable religious system for twentieth-century, educated, intellectual Jews. And one can see this thought dominating the ministry of the present Chief Rabbi, Dr Jonathan Sacks. The problem is that *Halachah* developed as an ancient system, was codified in medieval times, and has been accused of being utterly irrelevant to this generation. Sacks talks about '*Halachic* man', and asks the question, 'How can Halachic man remain true in such a different age?'[37]

Perceptively, he points out that there is a fundamental contradiction between *Halachah* and autonomy, which is today's prevalent philosophy. 'Autonomy,' he says, is 'the idea that each person is the author of his moral commitments.' This is totally hostile to the *Halachic* view, 'namely that we are born into obligations'.[38] Autonomy promotes the idea that one has the right, even the responsibility, to *choose* the way one will go; *Halachah* expresses that way in terms of directive–of law. Personal choice is not an option. The modern obsession with freedom and personal autonomy makes it very difficult for thinking people to submit to the *Halachic* way of life, and this has had a profound effect on the Jewish community.

Chief Rabbi Sacks is realistic about this problem. But although he recognises the need for, as he puts it, 'a mature Halachic response to the many pressing ethical, social and political questions of our time,' he also must surely realise that change is extremely difficult to achieve. Although *Halachah* itself developed to meet new situations and new needs, it has now become set in stone, and many orthodox Jews believe that, as a member of my own family affirmed, '*Halachah* cannot change.' The need, for Jewry, is glaring and pressing. Chief Rabbi Sacks faces no easy task.

Christians also have had problems, when situations have arisen which seemed not to be covered by the written

Scriptures. Hence we have Paul writing to the Corinthians about a specific problem: 'I say this (I, not the Lord)' (1 Corinthians 7:12).

Messianic *Halachah*?

The New Testament was, of course, written in Greek, whose concepts differ from those of Hebrew. But we need to remember that most of the early Christians *thought* in Hebrew concepts, even though those thoughts have come down to us expressed in an alien language. Jesus the Messiah, in fulfilment of prophecy (Isaiah 40:3), had a way prepared before him to walk in (John 1:23). John the Baptist's own parents had been described as 'observing all the Lord's commandments' (literally, 'walking in all the commandments') (Luke 1:6).

Jesus described himself as 'the way' (*ha derech*), saying frequently, 'Follow me.' As his disciples follow him, they are following the Rabbinic tradition of *Halachah*. Only this Rabbi is not as other rabbis! This thought is present also in the early tradition of calling Christians the 'followers of the Way' (Acts 9:2). One is reminded of the ancient wording, '*Uv'lecht'cha vaderech*' ('When thou walkest in the way') (Deuteronomy 6:7).

The word 'walk' is often used in the New Testament. A righteous man is described as one who was '[walking] in the fear of the Lord' (Acts 9:31). Paul directed his churches to 'walk in the footsteps of the faith' (Romans 4:12); to '[walk according] to this rule' (Galations 6:16) and, similarly, to 'walk by the same rule' (Philippians 3:16). He was accustomed to thinking of the right way of conducting oneself as a 'walk'–*Halachah*. But his argument in the letter to the Galatians makes it clear that he has no time for the legalistic interpretation of *Halachah* any more than Jesus himself had when he berated men for setting the traditions of men above the words of God (Mark 7:8).

The dilemma of Chief Rabbi Sacks, however, also faces Christians to some extent. We too are caught up in our cultural past and our own generation's way of thinking. We also are faced with two completely different sets of mores, though we often try to pretend this is not so. Paul put his finger on this when he warned the Colossian believers (largely Gentile), 'See to it that no-one takes you captive through hollow and deceptive philosophy, which depends on human tradition and the basic principles of this world rather than on [Messiah].' (Colossians 2:8).

There are things that the Bible says are wrong, and the world says are right. Christian '*Halachic* man/woman' will submit to the way of life promulgated by the Scriptures, walked by Jesus the Messiah, followed and taught by the apostles. *Halachah* has shaped what Jewish people have become. The path we walk, the way we conduct ourselves, will shape what we, and our children, become.

The man whose story opened this chapter came to walk in the way of Messiah Jesus at the age of forty-seven. At the end of a long life–ears failing, sight dim, walking unsteady, hands gnarled and stiff, he wrote these words:

> God be in my ears
> And in my hearing;
> God be in my feet
> Walking and running,
> Steadily standing;
> God be in my hands
> And in their doing;
> God keep clear my eyes
> To guide my viewing,

> Each and every day,
> To keep me on his way.[39]

Notes

1 Rabbi Dr Louis Jacobs, *Jewish Law* (Behrman House, 1968), p.1.
2 Rev. Dr A. Cohen.
3 Rev. Dr A. Cohen, *Everyman's Talmud* (J.M. Dent and Sons Ltd., 1932), Introduction, p.xxxiv.
4 *The Jewish Encyclopedia* (Funk and Wagnalls Co., 1903).
5 Eric Lipson, *Approaching the Jew* (Wickliffe Press, 1966), p.3.
6 *The Jewish Encyclopedia.*
7 Eric Lipson. Unpublished.
8 Moses ben Maimon, or RaMBaM. Twelfth-century Talmudist, philosopher, astronomer and physician.
9 Joseph Caro. 1488–1575. The last great codifier of Rabbinical Judaism, in his *Shulchan Aruch*.
10 Eric Lipson. Unpublished.
11 Rabbi Michael Friedlander. Past Principal of Jews' College, London.
12 Rabbi Michael Friedlander, *The Jewish Religion* (Shapiro, Vallentine and Co., 1922), p.138.
13 *A Rabbinic Anthology* (Macmillan and Co., Ltd., 1938), Introduction, p.xvi.
14 Rabbi Dr Louis Jacobs, *op. cit.*, p.1.
15 Rabbi Dr Louis Jacobs, *Theology in the Responsa* (Routledge and Kegan Paul, 1975), p.344.
16 Gershom Scholem, *Messianism in the Talmudic Era* (KTAV Publishing House Inc., 1979), p.53.
17 Avoth 1:1.
18 Eric Lipson. Unpublished.
19 Avoth 1:1.
20 Eric Lipson. Unpublished.
21 A Tractate of the Talmud.

22 Rabbi Dr Jonathan Sacks. Currently Chief Rabbi of the United Hebrew Congregations of the British Commonwealth.

23 Rabbi Dr Jonathan Sacks, *Tradition in an Untraditional Age* (Vallentine, Mitchell, 1990), p.270.

24 '*The Talmud*'. The Steinsaltz Edition; Reference Guide. 1989; p.295.

25 Twentieth-century Jewish thinker.

26 Rabbi Dr Louis Jacobs, *Theology in the Responsa* (Routledge and Kegan Paul, 1975), p.270.

27 Talmud. Sab.115b.

28 *A Rabbinic Anthology*, Introduction, p.xciii.

29 Eric Lipson. Unpublished.

30 Eric Lipson. Unpublished.

31 Rev. Dr A. Cohen, Introduction, p.xxxiv.

32 *Ibid.*, Introduction, p.xxxiv.

33 Rev. Dr A. Cohen, *Berachot* (Cambridge University Press, 1921) Introduction, p.xxxiv.

34 *Everyman's Talmud*, Introduction, p. xxxv.

35 Rev. Dr A. Cohen, *Berachot*, Introduction, p. xxxii.

36 Rabbi Dr Louis Jacobs, *op. cit.*, p. x (Preface).

37 Rabbi Dr Jonathan Sacks, *op. cit.*

38 *Ibid.*, p.100.

39 Eric Lipson. Unpublished.

כפר

In my dream, I saw . . . .

The traveller drew near to the gates of the great city.
Weary, hesitant, would she really be allowed in? Hovering
in those age-long minutes between life and Life–the
interval we call 'dying'–she recalled the words she had
so often, so glibly, sung: 'Bold I approach the eternal
throne.' So many years she had followed the master; he
so faithful, she so flawed; he so free with forgiveness, she
so persistently unworthy.

'Lord, forgive me. I've failed you so often, so badly. I
never seemed to be able to be what I wanted to be. I sinned
again and again.'

God smiled. She *heard* him smile! It was the most
beautiful sound she had ever heard.

'Sin? What sin? *I have no record*!'

7

KAPHAR

כפר

Covering

The Hebrew root *kaphar* gives rise to a number of words which are translated in amazingly different ways in the English versions of the Hebrew Scriptures (Old Testament). The basic meaning of the root, according to the lexicon,[1] is 'cover', 'cover over'. We find it in the story of Noah, where God directs him to make a boat and cover it with 'pitch' (Genesis 6:14). When the Israelites went out to gather manna, they found it covering the ground like 'hoar frost' (Exodus 16:14). It is easy to see that in both these examples the word is being used to describe something that *covers*–the boat, and the ground. It is used for 'a young lion' (Judges 14:5), 'a village' (1 Samuel 6:18) and 'a bowl' (Ezra 1:10). This requires a little more imagination, but perhaps we can say that, yes, a young lion straddles over its prey, after the kill, thus *covering* it; a village does *cover* an area of land; and the bowls used in Temple worship were plated–*covered*–with precious metals. In such ways do languages develop!

'It is traditional practice for the head to be covered in the presence of a scroll of the Law and, indeed, wherever Scripture is quoted in private, when prayers and blessings are said, and during religious study.'[2] Jewish men will often carry a skull cap in their pocket in order to be ready for these occasions. It is customary to provide them for the guests at many functions. The more pious wear them at all times. This cap, formerly known in the Yiddish vernacular as a 'koppel', is nowadays called a 'kippa'–a covering.

Atonement

In Exodus 30, *kaphar* is used in three different ways: 1) The covering–the lid–that was to be placed on the ark of the testimony in the most holy place is described as the 'atonement cover'. Older translations called this 'the Mercy-seat' (v.6). 2) Speaking of the annual sacrificial blood that was to be offered on the horns of the golden altar of incense, God said: 'This annual "atonement" must be made with the blood of the atoning sin offering' (v.10). 3) Every adult male counted in the census was required to give a 'ransom' of half a shekel (v.12), which would be considered as 'atonement money . . . 'making atonement' for their lives (v.16).

Here we see *kaphar* being used in connection with the problem caused by sin. There is the idea of 'substitution': the blood–the half shekel–would be accepted by God *in place of* something, or someone, else. 'A substitute of one kind or another was always meant (Psalm 48:, Isaiah 43:3–4).'[3] This concept of 'atonement' was going to have as its focal point the 'atonement cover', housed in the most holy place, and only to be approached, with the utmost reverence and care, once a year by the appointed high priest.

Reconciliation

The Jewish Encyclopedia defines *kaphar* as 'the setting at one, or reconciliation, of two estranged parties.' There is a sense in which 'appeasement', 'pacification', is implied: 'A king's wrath is a messenger of death, but a wise man will appease it' (Proverbs 16:14). There is a *covering over* of the cause of anger, a 'passing over' one's palm–ie a rubbing out. Rather as we speak of washing our hands of something. Jacob said of his coming confrontation with Esau: *'Akhapp'rah phanav'*–'I will cover his face', 'I will pacify him' (Genesis 32:20). Rashi commented on this text: 'I am of the opinion that wherever the verb KPhR is used in association with iniquity and sin and in association with "pannim" ("anger", "face"), it always signifies wiping away, removing.'

Forgiveness

In relation to God, humankind is estranged by its sin, and can only be reconciled by forgiveness–the sin being 'wiped away': 'When we were overwhelmed by sins, you forgave our transgressions' (Psalm 65:3). Our sin has made us guilty. Our guilt has raised a barrier between us and a holy God. Isaiah knew the problem: 'Woe to me . . . I am a man of unclean lips' (Isaiah 6:5). The sin needs to be *forgiven*. The guilt needs to be *purged.* The matter needs to be *covered over*, relegated to the past, forgotten, obliterated. That is the meaning of 'atonement'. 'Your guilt is taken away and your sin atoned for' (Isaiah 6:7).

Yom ha Kippurim

This, according to *The Jewish Encyclopedia*, was the original title of the Day of Atonement, Yom Kippur being a later, Rabbinic title. It was given to Israel to be the day of 'covering', 'forgiveness'; God's provision for his people's helplessness. The biblical ritual is described fully in Leviticus 16. Other sacrifices were offered on other days, but central to this day was the bringing of the two goats. One was killed and the blood offered; the other, the 'scapegoat', was dealt with quite differently. It was sent away into the wilderness–where exactly is not clear, though the tradition is that it was thrown from a high cliff. Until this had been testified as accomplished, no atonement was assured. The two together represent the full meaning of 'atonement': the blood offering says that sin has been covered, forgiven; the 'scapegoat' says that sin has been taken away, forgotten. Atonement is an utterly comprehensive way of dealing with sin and its consequent alienation of the sinner from God.

'The atoning blood actually meant the bringing about of a reunion with God, the restoration of peace between the soul and its Maker.'[4] 'God no longer hides his eyes from the sinner, because the sin has been covered.'[5] Blood was the essential ingredient; provided by God, to be offered by man: 'I have given it to you,' says God, 'to make atonement for yourselves' (Levitius 17:11). So it is that the 'most holy place' ('holy of holies') became known as *Bet ha-Kapporet*–the house, or place, of atonement (1 Chronicles 28:11).

If there is no Temple

This whole provision for atonement presupposed the existence of the Tabernacle/Temple, in the place of God's choosing. Imagine the desolation when that Temple was destroyed. Is atonement, then, no longer available? Joshua ben Hananiah expresses the sense of desolation: 'Woe unto us! Who shall atone for us?'[6]

The destruction of the Temple in AD 70, and the ensuing scattering of the Jewish people into the Diaspora, was catastrophic. But it seemed that some provision had already been made for this eventuality. Jochanan ben Zakkai had earlier been smuggled out of Jerusalem in a coffin and had gathered a group of disciples around him at Jabneh, a few miles from Jaffa. 'When news came that the Temple was burnt, the rabbis at Jabneh rent their garments. Rabbi Jochanan comforted another rabbi: "My son, be not cast down. We still have a means of atonement higher than sacrifice, chesed, the deeds of loving-kindness."'[7,8] Since that time there has been a divergence of practice and even theology concerning atonement.

Kapparot

This is a ceremony still practised in some Eastern communities. On the eve of Yom Kippur a cock is killed for a man, a hen for a woman. The words said are: *Zeh Kapparati*–this is my atonement . . . This fowl goeth to death whereas I am entering and going to a long life of goodness and peace . . . This be my substitute, this my exchanged sacrifice, this be my exchanged atonement.' There is no act of confession, as in the biblical requirement (Leviticus 16:21) but, perhaps instead, the bird is held in the right hand and the left hand placed on its head. It is then waved three times over the person, who recites: '*Nephesh tachat nephesh*–Life for life,' followed by Psalm 107:14,17–21 and Job 33:23–24: 'Spare him from going down to the pit; I have found a ransom for him.'

'This ritual appealed especially to Kabbalists.[9] The custom became general among the Jews of eastern Europe.'[10] But this idea of a vicarious sacrifice is not popular in mainstream Judaism. 'It has been strongly opposed . . . as a pagan one in conflict with the spirit of Judaism.'[11]

In Rabbinic Judaism

The massive dislocation caused by the destruction of the Temple had to be dealt with–and in no area was that more important than in the matter of atonement. Must we carry the burden of our sins to the grave, now that there can be no sacrifices? Or should we join this new sect of the Nazarene, who see atonement in the death of their founder? Surely not, argued the Rabbis. In the absence of sacrifice, we can rely upon the mercy of God. And so, over the years, a whole new theology of atonement developed with, 'for its constituent element: a) on the part of God, fatherly love and forgiving mercy; b) on the part of man, repentance and reparation of wrong.'[12]

Today, if truth be known, most Jewish people find the whole idea of animal sacrifices utterly repugnant and would not welcome their reintroduction, despite the fact that 'Orthodox Judaism remains Temple and Jerusalem centred; for the rebuilding of the Temple and the restoration of the sacrifices Jews pray thrice daily, and Jerusalem is remembered at every grace after meals.'[13] God, it is believed, 'maintains with His people an intimate covenant relationship' even though they 'are unable to offer the sacrifices prescribed in the Torah at the Sanctuary in Jerusalem.'[14] God Himself prays daily, 'May My mercy overcome My attribute of justice.'[15] If man cleaves to the good inclination rather than the bad, God will accept him. 'This principle sustains also the Liberal, Reform or Progressive Jew who does not expect or desire Temple restoration and rejects the validity of many Mosaic and, of course, Rabbinic laws.'[16]

Other factors can help. Some have taught that atonement can be achieved by suffering, by exile–above all, by death; particularly by the sufferings of Israel at the hands of persecutors. Israel Zangwill brought this out in *Dreamers of the Ghetto.*[17] Aaron the pedlar has caught the vision of his people's return to the land. 'Surely,' he says, 'The Jews must win back their country . . . then should the atonement of Israel be accomplished.'

Above all else, the Day of Atonement itself came to fill the void–itself effecting atonement,[18] though only if it is entered into with humility and proper repentance.[19] Without that, the day avails nothing. Prayer and good works too are required, though they also are valueless without repentance.[20]

On this day Israelites have been enjoined to 'deny themselves', or 'afflict their soul' (Leviticus 23:32). They do indeed fast, without food or water, from before sunset till after sunset, and they do spend many hours in synagogue in confession and contrition. This is the last of the Ten Days of Repentance which began on *Rosh Hashanah.* At the end of the day, it is hoped that God will have regarded his people mercifully and favourably:

> Lo, As the potter mouldeth plastic clay
> To forms his varying fancy doth display;
> So in Thy hand, O God of love, are we:
> Thy bond regard, let sin be veiled from Thee.[21]

'The atonement–sacrifices . . . except in the earliest parts of the Talmudic period, were a thing of the past. In their place the synagogue ritual of the Day of Atonement became in the popular mind the supreme path to the purification from sin. Its power to effect this is a tenet of Rabbinic Judaism.'[22]

Jesus the *Kapporet*

The Christian interpretation of 'atonement' is based on that taught in the Hebrew Scriptures. For these Scriptures, no *theological* difficulty is posed by the destruction of the Temple. Rather the reverse, in fact. The position is that Jesus was the perfect and eternal fulfilment of that teaching–the reality of what was but a shadow, because it could never be perfectly and permanently effective (Hebrews 10:1–18). 'Here I am,' he said. 'It is written about me in the scroll' (Hebrews 10:7; Psalm 40:6–8). 'We have been made holy through the sacrifice of the body of Jesus [the Messiah] once for all' (Hebrews 10:10). Because Jesus was perfect and eternal, his sacrifice, unlike those of *Yom ha Kippurim*, has no need to be repeated year after year. God now says, 'Their sins and lawless acts I will remember no more' (Hebrews 10:18; Jeremiah 31:34). 'Where these have been forgiven, there is no longer any sacrifice for sin' (Hebrews 10:18).

Isaiah 53

The Rabbinic and Christian views on atonement, therefore, are at variance. And nowhere is this seen more clearly than in the interpretation of Isaiah 53—the song of the suffering servant. The Jewish position is that the servant is Israel. Christians believe the servant is the Messiah Jesus. The two sides have become totally entrenched. Jews are forearmed against tract-bearing evangelists, their answer at the ready.

Christians believe that that this chapter is deliberately omitted from synagogue reading for ulterior motives. (In fact, many other prophetical passages are also omitted from the lectionary, those included having been chosen because they are appropriate as the *Haftarah*[23] to follow the day's *Torah* portion.) Perhaps it is time we started listening to each other. Beliefs are not formed in a vacuum; they grow in an environment of experiences and memories. For example, that siren I heard in Jerusalem meant 'war' to me, and 'peace' to the Israelis. But why? The answer is obvious. Now, stand in the place of 'the other side' as you consider Isaiah 53.

Against millennia of Israel's corporate experience and memories, *of course* Jewish people will see Israel as the suffering servant. How else do they make sense of their history? If suffering can be seen to be 'redemptive', it is so much easier to bear. Christians come from quite a different place. They are likely to feel an enormous sense of gratitude for the love God has shown them, as undeserving individuals, in sending his Son to die on the cross–for them, personally. They may have experienced the lifting of an unbearable load as they contemplated that cross. *Of course* it is obvious, to them, that the servant is Jesus. How could anyone not see it? Perhaps we sometimes force an 'either/or' confrontation in scenarios where God is offering a 'both/and' solution.

The cross

John could say, using the language of the translators of the Septuagint,[24] 'Jesus [the Messiah] . . . is the atoning sacrifice (Greek–*hilasterion*, Hebrew–*kapporet*) for our sins, and not only for ours but also for the sins of the whole world' (1 John 2:2). 'This is love: not that we loved God, but that he loved us and sent his Son as an atoning sacrifice for our sins' (1 John 4:10).

This means that the cross is central to Christianity. It represents, for Christians, the love of God for all human-kind. It needs to be remembered that the cross means something totally different for Jews. 'The "offence of the cross" is twofold. The cross offends all who are unwilling to put their faith in Christ . . . and it offends also all for whom it represents sinful, unloving man's inhumanity, particularly towards the lost sheep of the house of Israel to whom Jesus himself was sent, and to whom he sent his disciples.'[25]

The crusades are particularly remembered, as whole Jewish communities were terrorised by persecutors decorated with emblazoned crosses. 'There are two ends to a spear. While Christian knights handled the butt end, the Jew was acquainted only with the point.'[26] Christians would do well to learn from their Jewish friends that the atonement is not an abstract dogma but an act of love. On our part it requires, as well as faith, repentance, prayer and good works. Thus will faith be seen to be genuine.

Notes

1 Brown, Driver and Briggs.
2 Eric Lipson. Unpublished.
3 Walter C. Kaiser, Jr, *Toward an Old Testament Theology* (Zondervan, 1978), p.117.
4 *The Jewish Encyclopedia* (Funk and Wagnalls Co., 1903).
5 Eric Lipson. Unpublished.
6 *The Jewish Encyclopedia.*
7 Avoth D'Rabbi Nathan C. 4.
8 Eric Lipson. Unpublished.
9 An esoteric, mystical sect whose origins went back at least to Apocryphal times. Simeon ben Yochai (second century) is said complied its fundamental book, the *Zohar.*
10 *The Jewish Encyclopedia.*

11 *The Jewish Encyclopedia.*
12 *Ibid.*
13 Eroc Lipson, *Approaching the Jew* (Wickliffe Press, 1966), p.3.
14 *Ibid.*, p. 1.
15 Ber.7a.
16 Eric Lipson, *op. cit.*, p. 3.
17 Israel Zangwill, *Dreamers of the Ghetto* (Heinemann, 1898), p.407.
18 *The Jewish Encyclopedia.*
19 Yoma 8:8.
20 *Service of the Synagogue* (Routledge), Day of Atonement, vol. 2, pp.149–150.
21 From an anonymous poem, included in the liturgy for *Kol Nidre*–the eve of Yom Kippur.
22 Rev. Dr A. Cohen, *Everyman's Talmud* (J.M. Dent and Sons Ltd., 1932), p.114.
23 *Haftarah*–literally, 'conclusion'. That portion of the prophets read in synagogue immediately after the *Torah.*
24 Septuagint. Greek translation of the Hebrew Scriptures, dating from the later centuries before the birth of Jesus.
25 Eric Lipson, *op. cit.*, p. 8.
26 Israel Abrahams, ed., *Jewish Life in the Middle Ages* (Cecil Roth. Edward Goldston Ltd., 1932), p.185.

תְּשׁוּבָה

'How could this be happening to me?'

All he'd ever wanted was to be a good Jew–practising the religion of his fathers, raising his children in a God-fearing environment, fully involved in the life of the synagogue. So where had it all gone wrong? Years of *tsurus* (aggravation) in a disfunctional marriage; now wife and children gone. Devastation, humiliation, a searing sense of loss. Anger. 'How could she do this to me–to the children?'

A 'chance' visit to a little Regency church in London led to friendship with Jakob Jocz, an Anglican clergyman who could say, 'I also am a Jew': the one man who could have understood, helped; who was prepared to give unstintingly of listening hours. Only a few months later understanding broke through.

'I suppose what really matters is not so much what has been done to me, as where I myself have gone wrong.'

'Yes–you must become a *baal teshuvah*–a master of repentance. A penitent.'

8

TESHUVAH
תשובה

The Rabbis say

'Sin,' taught the Rabbis, 'first appears as a frail spider's web, growing as tough as a cable; whereas a touch will free us from its entanglement in the early stages, later only the mightiest efforts can free us from its bonds.'[1] 'But no human being is so bad as to be absolutely irredeemable. Nor should any be so complacent as to regard themselves as perfect. They should be honest and realistic and see themselves as they really are–'part guilty and part innocent' is the Talmudic phrase. 'The way of ensuring God's favour is that of repentance. It implies a conscious effort to turn away from evil-doing and bad habits and a return to the service of God. No man whose repentance is really sincere– even though it comes at the eleventh hour–will be rejected by God,' said Raymond Apple in his 'Companion' to the *Yom Kippur* liturgy. He quoted Isaiah 55:7: 'Let the wicked forsake his way, and the man of iniquity his thoughts, and let him return to the Lord, and he will have compassion upon him, and to our God, for he will abundantly pardon.'[2]

'Repent one day before your death,' said Rabbi Eliezer,[3] according to the *Talmud*.[4] 'How does a man know when he is to die?' asked the Rabbi's pupils, falling right into the trap! 'Then repent each day,' was his reply.

Repentance atones for sin

Teshuvah (repentance) is a concept of such importance that it is reputed to be one of seven things which were created before the universe came into being[5], as if creation would not be sustainable without it. God, in his graciousness, prepared in advance the remedy for the fall which, in his foreknowledge, he foresaw. It is one of three things which can turn God himself away from judgement upon sin. As the *Talmud* says: 'Three things avert the evil decree: Tefillah (prayer), Teshuvah (repentance) and Tzedakah (almsgiving).'[6] And, 'Repentance and good works are as a shield in the face of punishment.'[7]

Belief in sin and punishment are deeply embedded in the Hebrew Scriptures (Old Testament) and in Rabbinic Judaism, although humanity is said to be 'part good, part bad' rather than totally depraved. Because sin is seen to erect a barrier between God and humanity–a barrier described so graphically in the story of the fall in Genesis–it became necessary to find a way of breaking down that barrier. God desires it. Men and women, at their highest, long for it. And the barrier can only be broken down by means of forgiveness. So, how to find forgiveness? The *Torah* teaches, in the early chapters of Leviticus, that God himself prescribed the way through the sacrificial system, which Christians see as foretelling, in type, the sacrifice of God's Son, Jesus, on the cross.

But if your Temple is destroyed, the sacrifices (only legitimately offered at 'the place of God's choosing') no longer possible, and you do not accept the possibility of a crucified Messiah–what then? It is necessary to find another way. The people cannot be left without hope of forgiveness. And that way is repentance. Rabbi Cohen says, in *Everyman's Talmud*: 'There are various ways by which a sinner can atone for his wrongdoing, and the chief of these is repentance.'[8] That is why, he says, there is still the possibility of forgiveness, even without the Temple and the sacrifices.

Repentance–what is it?

It is necessary to consider what *teshuvah* actually is. It is much more than a mere 'feeling sorry'. The literal meaning is 'turning'. Repentance, for the Jew, consists of four elements: 1) consciousness of sin, according to Ecclesiastes 7:20; 2) confession: to God, and to those against whom we have offended; 3) regret: of the evil done and of the good left undone; 4) amendment. All these elements are dealt with in the liturgy for *Yom Kippur* (the Day of Atonement), when Jewry fasts and prays for the slate to be wiped clean. Many will have previously visited the *Mikveh* (ritual bath) as a symbolic act of the washing away of sin. As Maimonides[9] said: 'What is teshuvah? It is this: that the sinner abandons his sin, removes it from his thoughts and resolves in his heart never to repeat it . . . Also he should regret the past, as it is said: "After I returned, I regretted."'[10] The *Talmud* also says: 'For transgressions between man and his neighbour Yom Kippur does not procure forgiveness until he first appeases his neighbour.'[11]

This is why *Yom Kippur* is preceded by ten days of repentance, commencing on *Rosh Hashanah*–New Year (in biblical times, the Festival of Trumpets). It is customary, during these days, to go around restoring relationships

which have become broken during the course of the year–
apologising, making amends. My husband, who always
fasted and attended synagogue on *Yom Kippur*, used to
say, 'Fasting becomes a farce unless we are truly humbled
as we stand before God in judgement.' There is a firm
belief that, if the conditions are met, God does indeed
forgive. As M.L. Margolis[12] wrote: 'I believe that he who
confesses his sins and turns from his evil ways and truly
repents is lovingly forgiven by his Father in heaven.'[13] The
problem is, of course, that one can never be absolutely
certain that one has adequately repented.

Repentance, if genuine, will involve change. The Bible
speaks of 'turning', and 'returning' (Malachi 3:7 and
Ezekiel 33:11). There has to be a determination not to
repeat the offence. 'A person who says, "I shall sin and
repent . . .' no opportunity to repent will be afforded him
. . . if he says, "I shall sin and Yom Kippur will procure
forgiveness", then Yom Kippur will not procure forgiveness.'[14] The liturgy for *Yom Kippur* includes the prayer:
'May it be Thy will, O Lord my God and the God of my
fathers, that I may sin no more.' And Rabbi Judah taught,
'Who is the penitent man? The man who, when the same
opportunity for sin occurs once or twice, refrains from
sinning.'[15]

Repentance is liberating

Chief Rabbi Jonathan Sacks[16] picks up this idea of 'turning' when he says, 'Teshuvah insists that we can liberate
ourselves from our past, defy predictions of our future by
a single act of turning–as long as we do it now.'[17] To
Sacks, the concept of 'now' is all important. He cites the
words of Moses, '*Now*, O Israel, what does God your Lord
ask of you?' The sages, he says, add a cryptic comment:

'The word "now" means nothing other than "teshuvah".
'Tomorrow', he says, 'is the enemy of teshuvah.'

Chief Rabbi Sacks tackles head-on the modern escape
route of inheritance and environment as excuses for our
sins. To hide from reality in this way, he claims, is to
submit to slavery. Repentance is the God-given path which
liberates us from bondage to both our conditioning and
our inheritance. We are not trapped by genetics or
environment any more than by the influence of the stars.
That kind of thinking is a retreat from both responsibility
and freedom. All are free to change, to repent. What a
welcome breath of fresh air his thinking is! Would that
more Church leaders were speaking in these terms. He sees
repentance as positive and active, reconstructing the
broken personality–essentially creative.

Repentance is healing

'Great is repentance for it brings healing to the world. Great
is repentance for it reaches to the Throne of Glory. Great is
repentance for it makes the Redemption (ie by the Messiah)
to come near. Great is repentance for it lengthens the years
of a man's life.'[18] Repentance reaches the ready heart of
God. Rabbinic tradition has it that God himself prays,
'May my attribute of mercy overcome my attribute of
wrath.'[19] There is a lovely prayer in the liturgy for *Kol
Nidre*[20]: '*Thou hast given us in love*, O Lord our God, this
Day of Atonement for pardon, forgiveness and atonement.'
This is not something we have to drag ourselves to do for a
harsh, exacting God–he has given it to us, out of his heart of
love, because he longs for the renewal of fellowship with us,
for the barrier to be broken down.

In *A Rabbinic Anthology* there is a story redolent of
Luke 15: 'A king had a son who had gone astray from his

father ... His friends said to him, "Return to your father"; He said, "I cannot". Then his father sent to say, "Return as far as *you* can, and *I* will come to you the rest of the way." So God says, "Return to Me, and I will return to you."'[21]

It is not to be thought that repentance is a bitter experience. Not only is it liberating, as Chief Rabbi Sacks teaches, it is also 'sweet': 'Sweeter is one hour of repentance and good deeds than all the life of the world to come.'[22] Surely that sweetness comes from the lifting of the burden of guilt, the restoration of fellowship–with God and with others, the knowledge that one is a *baal teshuvah*–starting afresh, and that there is no need to repeat the old mistakes. Nothing is inevitable.

This is truly healing. That is why Isidore Epstein[23] wrote, commenting on Isaiah 58:6–9: 'Although the Day of Atonement is a day of fasting and repentance, it is not a day given over to gloom and sadness ... it is ... a day which brings with it the glad tidings of God's pardon and forgiveness, and the opportunity for each one of us to start a new life, without the feeling of misery for what we may have done or failed to do in the past.'[24] Repentance and forgiveness mean that one can walk tall, without the stress of guilt which so drags one down. Truly, as the *Talmud* says, repentance is a healing gift.[25]

Corporate repentance

Provision is made, in Leviticus 4, for corporate repentance. There is a moment during the Passover *Seder* when a drop of wine is taken from our cups for each of the plagues. This is to symbolise the lessening of our joy because of the sufferings of the Egyptians. Chief Rabbi Sacks makes an appeal for this to be developed as a way of expressing corporate repentance. Even in our righteous struggles there should be sorrow for hurt inflicted.

Repentance must be wholehearted

'When you and your children return to the Lord your God and obey him with all your heart and with all your soul . . . then the Lord your God will restore' (Deuteronomy 30:2–3). The Bratzlaver[26] spoke of the total experience of repentance: 'There are three requisites for repentance: seeing eyes, hearing ears, and an understanding heart, ready to return and be healed. Let your eyes see your conduct; your ears hear words of admonition . . . and let your heart understand its eternal purpose. Then you will attain perfect penitence.'[27] And Rabbi Sussya of Anipol[28] said

> There are five verses in the Bible which constitute the essence of Judaism. These verses begin with the Hebrew letters: Tav, Shin, Vav, Beth, Heh; which comprise the Hebrew word for repentance: 'teshuvah':
>
>> Thou shalt be wholehearted with the Lord thy God' (Deuteronomy 18:13);
>> 'I have set the Lord always before me' (Psalm 16:8);
>> 'But thou shalt love thy neighbour as thyself' (Leviticus 19:18);
>> 'In all thy ways acknowledge Him' (Proverbs 3:6);
>> 'To walk humbly with thy God' (Micah 6:8).
>
> Therefore, 'Resolve to act accordingly, so that your repentance may be sincere.'[29]

Repentance, if sincere and acceptable, will be wholehearted; it will be God-centred; it will involve a putting right of relationships, and it will be humble; it will result in a changed way of life.

The Hebrew Scriptures say

Teshuvah *leads to blessing*

The thinking of the Rabbis is developed largely from Scripture. In Deuteronomy 30:1–10 we see a God who, foreseeing in advance the people's inevitable failure, tells them that he has prescribed the remedy–'When you . . . return to the Lord your God and obey him with all your heart . . . then the Lord your God will restore your fortunes and have compassion on you.' The key is 'returning'–*teshuvah*; repentance which is wholehearted, which involves change, will always be followed by restoration. Walter Kaiser points out that 'repentance (in Deuteronomy 30) has a counter theme: Israel was offered the blessing, promise and assurance of God.'[30]

Samuel highlighted this thought when the people had been mourning the loss of the ark for twenty years: 'If you are returning to the Lord with all your hearts, then rid yourselves of the foreign gods . . . commit yourselves to the Lord and serve him only, and he will deliver you' (1 Samuel 7:3). One can almost say that 'repent' sums up the message of the prophets and seers of Israel (2 Kings 17:13). And when King Josiah was given the highest accolade of all the kings, it was in these words: 'Neither before nor after Josiah was there a king like him who *turned* to the Lord as he did–with all his heart and with all his soul and with all his strength, in accordance with all the Law of Moses' (2 Kings 23:25, my italics).

When there is a new work of God after a time of failure, *teshuvah*–turning, repentance–is the key. Refusal to repent is seen as another kind of turning–turning away (Jeremiah 8:5). So lack of repentance is an active, not a passive, sin.

The prophet Joel wrote that *teshuvah* would trigger the demonstration of that most beautiful of God's attributes–*chesed*: gracious, merciful, lovingkindness (Joel 2:13). He is by nature compassionate and forgiving, but he is also holy, righteous. When his people are in sin there has to be either *teshuvah* or judgement–or God himself is no longer credible. But the response to *teshuvah* will be blessing. This is the pattern, seen earlier, in David's song of repentance (Psalm 51). The background story is recorded in 1 Samuel 11 and 12. David came in deep contrition (v.17), appealing to God's unfailing *chesed*–covenant love (v.1). And, on the basis of that contrition and that love, he dared to ask God to recreate, renew and restore him (vv.10–12). That would be transformation indeed; God's own work in his life, fulfilling the need for true repentance to be demonstrated by change. Only then, David realised, could he offer acceptable worship (vv.15–17).

Shallow teshuvah *is not acceptable*

One could almost say that Hosea's prophecy is one long, heart-rending appeal for *teshuvah*. 'Come, let us *return* to the Lord . . . He will heal us . . . He will restore us, that we may live in his presence' (Hosea 6:1–2, my italics). Guilt is recognised, and God's justice in judgement; but also his healing power and his intense desire to exercise mercy. But shallow repentance is not acceptable. 'Take words,' he says, 'and *return* to the Lord' (Hosea 14:2, my italics). But words alone will not be enough. There must also be confession and then change. They must 'never again say "Our gods" to what [their] own hands have made' (Hosea 14:3). As Rabbi Cohen said in *The Soncino Commentary* on Hosea: 'The return to God must be complete and whole-hearted if it is to prove efficacious.'

Teshuvah with genuine determination to change will always meet with response; with healing and love (v.4); with abatement of anger; with restoration and blessing (vv.5–7). God is indeed so quick to respond to *teshuvah* that he can seem almost unfair–that is how Jonah felt about the Lord's dealings with Nineveh (Jonah 4:2).

Teshuvah *is a work of God's Spirit*

More than two centuries later, after Israel's return from exile, the call was still the same: '*Return* to me . . . and I will return to you' (Zechariah 1:3, my italics). God has not given up on his people, but he still demands *teshuvah*. Yet Zechariah also told of a day when God himself would pour a spirit of repentance upon his people (Zechariah 13:1). They will mourn for the pierced Messiah. And God himself will remove the impurities from the land, and open to the house of David a fountain 'to cleanse them from sin and impurity' (13:1–2). So the Hebrew Scriptures draw to a close with a recognition that true *teshuvah* is a work of the Spirit of God himself.

The New Testament Scriptures say

A change of mind

The Greek word commonly translated as 'repentance' is *metanoia*–literally, 'a change of mind'. *The IVF New Bible Dictionary* says, 'Repentance consists in a radical transformation of thought, attitude, outlook and direction.' Part of this transformation will be to feel a hatred of the sin which was formerly cherished (2 Corinthians 7:9). Notice that sorrow alone is not in itself repentance; sorrow for sin *leads* to repentance, which in turn leads to salvation (v.10) and then to a change in outlook (v.11). It is not enough only to feel–or even express–sorrow and regret.

A turning

Another word altogether gives the Hebrew thought of *teshuvah*–'turning': *epistrepho*–commonly translated as 'to convert'. So Jesus said to Peter, seeing his coming failure and betrayal, 'When you have "converted" (or "turned back"), strengthen your brothers' (Luke 22:32). And Peter himself taught, 'Repent . . . turn to God' (Acts 3:19). Here are the Hebrew and Greek concepts in tandem: 'repent' (change your outlook) and 'turn' (change your ways). True, complete, acceptable repentance can never be only intellectual, though it must be that. It must be heartfelt brokenness, a determination to change; and it must lead to action–to transformation; lasting transformation.

Repentance–forgiveness–salvation

John the Baptist linked repentance with forgiveness and salvation, quoting the prophet Isaiah. But he also demanded change–radical change (Luke 3:1–18)! As he saw it, nothing superficial, purely verbal or ritual was acceptable.

Jesus' public ministry began with a call to 'Repent' (Matthew 4:17), linking the need for repentance with his 'kingdom' teaching. 'Unless you turn, and become like little children, you will never enter the kingdom of heaven' (Matthew 18:3). Surely this is why repentance is precious to the Father: 'There will be . . . rejoicing in heaven over one sinner who repents' (Luke 15:7). Jesus' message was that God longs to welcome us into the kingdom and that we should find the entry-key–repentance. That was why he came: to call sinners to repentance.

There is a difference of emphasis here from that of the Rabbis, for whom the blessings of repentance are for this life, and not associated with the kingdom; that is seen as a purely future, Messianic age. Jesus' teaching is that, with his coming, the kingdom overlaps the present and the future–and the blessings of repentance are for more than this life only.

For Jesus, it seems, repentance and forgiveness were the beginning and end of the matter, no one being too gifted or respected to escape this challenge. And the Messiah's ministry on earth closed with the command that repentance and forgiveness of sins should be preached to all (Luke 24:47). Truly, repentance is at the heart of the Christian faith.

Notes

1 Sukkah 52a.
2 R. Raymond Apple, *Companion to the Machzor for Rosh Hashanah and Yom Kippur* (United Synagogue Pub. Committee, 1964), p.26.
3 Rabbi Eliezer Ben Hyrcanus. First and second century.
4 Shab.153a.
5 Pes.54a.
6 Pes.K.191a.
7 Avoth 4:13.
8 Rev. Dr A. Cohen, *Everyman's Talmud* (J.M. Dent and Sons Ltd., reprint 1937), p.112.
9 Moses Ben Maimon, or RaMBaM. Twelfth-century Talmudist, philosopher, astronomer and physician.
10 Teshuvah 5:2.
11 Yoma 8:9.
12 Early twentieth century. Professor of Semitic Languages, University of California.

13 *A Book of Jewish Thoughts* (Oxford University Press, 1920), p.22.

14 Yoma 8:9.

15 Yoma 86b.

16 Chief Rabbi of the United Hebrew Congregations of the British Commonwealth.

17 Rabbi Dr Jonathan Sacks, *Tradition in an Untraditional Age* (Vallentine, Mitchell, 1990), pp.203–204.

18 Yoma 86a ff.

19 Ber.7a.

20 The Eve of the Day of Atonement.

21 Montefiore and Loewe, *A Rabbinic Anthology* (Macmillan and Co., Ltd, 1938), p.321.

22 Avoth 4:22.

23 Principal of Jews' College, London, in the middle of this century.

24 Rabbi Dr Isidore Epstein, *Step By Step in the Jewish Religion* (Soncino Press, 1958), p.124.

25 Yoma 86a.

26 Chassidic writer. 1772–1810. Great grandson of the Besht. Considered by some as the greatest story-teller of the Jewish people.

27 *Likkutei Etsoth ha-Shalem.*

28 Chassidic Rabbi. Brother of the Lizensker. Died 1800.

29 Mif.H. p.49.

30 Walter C. Kaiser, jr, *Toward an Old Testament Theology* (Zondervan, 1978), p.139.

At the dawn I seek Thee,
Refuge, Rock sublime;
Set my prayer before Thee in the morning,
And my prayer at even-time.

I before Thy greatness
Stand, and am afraid;
All my secret thoughts Thine eye beholdeth,
Deep within my bosom laid.

And withal, what is it
Heart and tongue can do?
What is this my strength, and what is even
This my spirit in me, too?

But indeed man's singing
May seem good to Thee.
So I praise Thee, singing, while there dwelleth
Yet the breath of God in me.

Solomon ibn Gabirol, eleventh century
Translated by Nina Salaman

9

TEFILLAH

תפלה

The simple meaning of *tefillah* is 'prayer'. But, as is so often the case with Hebrew words and concepts, more is implied. There is a sense in which *tefillah* is a stepping of the whole person into the supernatural realm, beyond the limits of what can be perceived with the natural senses and achieved by the natural abilities. *The Jewish Encyclopedia* definition is: 'Thought, hope . . . as representing the means of discriminating between good and evil.' Rabbi Samson Raphael Hirsch[1] went deeper. The root meaning, he said, implies a stepping 'out of active life in order to attempt to gain a true judgment about oneself . . . about one's relationship to God and the world, and of God and the world to oneself.'[2]

The root of the word is *palal*–'to judge', and the form of this root used for 'prayer' is reflexive, so one could say that 'the meaning of "to pray" in Hebrew is literally "to judge oneself". Prayer, tefillah, implies self-examination.'[3]

However, lest it should be thought that *tefillah* is so deeply spiritual–mystical, even–as to be beyond the ordinary person, Jewish teaching is that this is by no means so.

God 'has endowed us with a natural impulse to pray'.[4] All (even women!) are enjoined to pray, and–given the right attitudes and conditions–their prayers will be heard and answered.

The importance of prayer

'Prayer became all-important when the Temple was destroyed and all sacrifices ceased.'[5] Some means had to be found to provide for the forgiveness of sins, now that the sacrifices could no longer be offered. So the teaching developed that prayer, sincerely offered, (together with repentance and charity) is one of the means of 'averting the evil decree'. As Rabbi Isaac said, 'We have now no prophet or priest or sacrifices or Temple, or altar which can make atonement for us: from the day whereon the Temple was laid waste, nought was left to us but prayer. Therefore, O God, hearken and forgive.'[6]

From this teaching, arising out of necessity, it is but a short step to declare that 'prayer is valued higher than sacrifice'.[7] Indeed–'greater is prayer than good deeds.'[8] Moses achieved more than any other in the nation's history, but even he achieved more by prayer than by his deeds: 'One hour in prayer is better than good works; not because of his good works was it said to Moses, "Go up and view the land," but because of his supplication.'[9]

But prayer is not considered to be the most important activity in the religious life. 'The obligation to pray is Rabbinic, not Biblical.'[10] It is more important to study *Torah*. Study is a biblical precept. 'He that turneth away his ear from hearing the Law, even his prayer shall be an abomination' (Proverbs 28:9).[11] Therefore *Torah* study must always take precedence over prayer. 'Raba, who observed Rabbi Hamnuna lingering over his prayers, remarked: "They put aside everlasting life (Torah) and concern themselves with the temporal life (praying for maintenance)."'[12]

The efficacy of prayer

'The belief in the objective efficacy of prayer is never questioned in the Bible.'[13] Exodus 8:29, 1 Kings 17:20, Jonah 3 and other references are quoted to support this statement. This belief is not seen to contradict the doctrine of the immutability of God's will. The fifth Principle of the Jewish Faith states: 'I firmly believe that the Creator, blessed be His Name, alone is worthy of being worshipped, and that no other being is worthy of our worship.' This principle 'implies the belief that God can fulfil our petitions. We believe in the efficacy of prayer.'[14] God is actively involved in the affairs of his creation. The basis of prayer is the idea of God's real and active role in the universe.[15]

The more mystical traditions see much more in this than the mere mechanics of our 'Please, Lord' and his 'Yes' or 'No'. It is as if, by prayer, the barrier between this world and the next is temporarily melted. The *Zohar* declares: 'When men in prayer declare the unity of the holy Name in love and reverence, the walls of earth's darkness are cleft in twain, and the face of the heavenly King is revealed, lighting up the universe.'[16]

On a more mundane level, it has been said that 'prayer is Israel's only weapon, a weapon inherited from their fathers, a weapon tried in a thousand battles'.[17] And just as every warrior needs to feel confidence in his weapons, so he who prays must exercise faith in the one to whom he prays. Faith is seen to be 'the principle upon which the whole relationship of man with God ultimately rests', and it is in the act of prayer that faith finds its truest expression.[18]

Faith in the God who answers prayer is particularly marked in the case of prayers for forgiveness. It has already been noted that, since the destruction of the Temple, prayer, together with repentance and charity, has replaced sacrifice as a means of averting God's wrath.

As the Scriptures promise, 'If My people . . . will humble themselves and pray . . . then will I hear from heaven and will forgive their sin and heal their land' (2 Chronicles 7:14). This is picturesquely expressed in the saying: 'Why is the prayer of the righteous like a rake? As the rake turns the grain from place to place, so the prayer of the righteous man turns the attributes of God from the attribute of wrath to the attribute of mercy.'[19]

Anyone who claims to believe in the efficacy of prayer has to find a way of explaining why some prayers appear to be unanswered. Christians also have this problem. And most Christians would have no difficulty with the Rabbis' explanation: if God seems not to be answering a prayer, it is 'because the request, if granted, would not have been for the asker's good. Indeed, it is a mark of the true Israelite not to murmur if the request be denied.'[20] Faith in God demands that one trusts not only in God's ability to answer prayer but also, ultimately, in God's all-seeing, all-loving wisdom: 'We pray to the Almighty, being convinced that it is in His power to grant what we pray for; but we must trust in the wisdom and mercy of God, that the rejection of our petition is also for our good.'[21] So prayer ought not to be arrogantly presumptuous: 'Do not make thy prayer a fixed claim or demand, which must be fulfilled, but a supplication for mercy, which may or may not be granted.'[22]

Spontaneous prayer

It is probably true to say that, nowadays, most Jewish prayer–whether public or private–is liturgical. But this has not always been the case. 'Prayer was . . . of a devotional character and entirely voluntary during the time of the First Temple. The regular daily prayers commenced after the destruction of the First Temple, when they replaced the sacrifices'[23] (Hosea 14:2). But this spirit of spontaneous prayer has remained a part of Jewry, particularly in the prayer-life of individuals. As Rabbi Eliezer said, 'If a man makes his prayer a fixed task (ie mechanical) his prayer is no supplication.'[24] This is true even in the case of the mandatory, regular prayers: 'Rabbi Simeon used to say: Be meticulous in reciting the Shema and the Tefillah. And when you pray, do not make your prayer a matter of routine, but a plea for God's mercy and grace.'[25]

In medieval times there was the rise of mysticism, bringing with it the desire to reach after God in a personal, even emotional, way. Some of the Jewish poetry of this period expresses these yearnings most beautifully. One example, which I keep hanging by my bed, is found at the beginning of this chapter. Here is another:

> My meditation day and night,
> May it be pleasant in Thy sight,
> For Thou art all my soul's delight.[26]

Intercession

Praying for others should always take precedence over praying for oneself. Abraham has been called 'the father of prayer' because of his intercession on behalf of others (Genesis 18): 'Abraham has been made by tradition the father of prayer . . . a prayer in the true sense of the word, not for himself but for his fellow-men. Abraham was the first who recognised God as Lord of man, in whose hand his fate lies–the condition sine qua non of prayer.'[27] Not to pray for others in need is culpable. 'Whoever has it in his power to pray on behalf of his neighbour and fails to do so, is called a sinner.'[28] As Samuel said to the people: 'Far be it from me that I should sin against the Lord by failing to pray for you' (1 Samuel 12:23).

In fact, prayer for others may even cause blessings to rebound on one's own head:

> Who for his neighbour's sake doth plead,
> That God to him a gift may send,
> If he himself that boon doth need,
> Receives that boon before his friend.[29]

Occasions for prayer

There are prayers for every possible occasion. The collection of these, in one book, is known as the *Seder Tefillot* (Order of Prayers) or, simply, the *Siddur*. This contains prayers for weekdays, Sabbaths, holy-days and fast-days throughout the year. The first known compilation of this sort was that of Amram Gaon in the ninth century.

The psalms have a prominent place in the prayer life of the congregation, and the predominant note is that of blessing and praise. Songs, too, have been composed over the centuries and found their way into the liturgy. In countless Jewish homes, to different melodies, *Shalom Aleychem* is sung in Hebrew every Friday evening:

> Peace be to you, ministering angels,
> Messengers of the Most High, of the Supreme Sovereign,
> The Holy One, ever to be praised.

Enter in peace, O messengers of the Most High,
Of the Supreme Sovereign,
The Holy One, ever to be praised.

Bless us with peace, O messengers of the Most High,
Of the Supreme Sovereign,
The Holy One, ever to be praised.

Depart in peace, O messengers of the Most High,
Of the Supreme Sovereign,
The Holy One, ever to be praised.

Songs can have the supplementary purpose of changing the tempo of what can be rather long proceedings. How many children, drooping long after normal bed-time on Passover night, have been jerked into a last fling of wakefulness when the strains of *Addir Hu* signal the final phase of the *Seder*:

God of might,
God of right,
Thee we give all glory.
Thine the praise,
In our days,
As in ages hoary.

When we hear,
Year by year,
Our redemption's story,
Now as erst,
When thou first
Mad'st the proclamation,
Warning loud,
Ev'ry proud,
Ev'ry tyrant nation,
We Thy fame
Still proclaim,
God of our salvation.

The theme of forgiveness has inspired many songs and poems. Here is one dating from the twelfth century, inspired by the liturgy for *Yom Kippur*:

> Raise to Thee, this my plea, take my prayer,
> Sin unmake for Thy sake and declare,
> 'Forgiven!'
>
> Tears, regret, witness set in sin's place;
> Uplift trust from the dust to Thy face–
> 'Forgiven!'
>
> Voice that sighs, tear-filled eyes, do not spurn;
> Weigh and pause, plead my cause, and return
> 'Forgiven!'
>
> Yea, off-rolled–as foretold–clouds impure,
> Zion's folk, free of yoke, O assure
> 'Forgiven!'[30]

Chanucah–the Festival of Dedication–is inseparably linked, in the minds of Jewish children, with lighted miniature candles, '*Chanucah gelt*' (for the lucky ones!) and *Maoz Tzur*:

> Refuge, Rock of my salvation,
> To You our praise is due.
> Let Your House become a House of prayer
> And thanksgiving for all peoples.
> When by your will all bloodshed ends
> And enemies cease to scream hate:
> Then we shall celebrate with joyful song
> The true dedication of Your altar.

Many prayers are blessings. Whereas a Christian host may ask an honoured guest to 'say grace', my husband would invite him to 'say a *berachah*' (blessing). 'Let not a man taste anything until he pronounces a benediction, for it is said: "The earth is the Lord's, and the fulness thereof, the world and they that dwell in it" (Psalm 24:1).'[31] There is a blessing to be said before and after food, over wine, on seeing a rainbow, catching the first sight of the sea, over the first fruit of a new season. Any occasion of special rejoicing will be greeted by the words, 'Blessed art thou, O Lord our God, King of the universe.'

There is a prayer for one about to set out on a journey, dating from days when travelling was a major undertaking: 'May it be Thy will, O Lord my God, to conduct me in peace, to direct my steps in peace, to uphold me in peace.'[32] One could find oneself in sudden danger, in need of a 'dart prayer'. In such a case, 'Rabbi Eliezer said: Do Thy will in heaven above; grant tranquility of spirit to those who fear Thee below, and do that which is good in Thy sight.'[33]

'From the earliest epochs recorded in the Bible profound distress or joyous exultation found expression in prayer.'[34] The Rabbis have always taught that the Lord is to be blessed at all times and on every occasion–in sorrow as well as in joy. Hence it is that in bereavement and on the anniversary of bereavement (the *Yahrzeit*) the *Kaddish* is recited by mourners: 'Blessed, praised and glorified, exalted, extolled and honoured, magnified and lauded be the Name of the Holy One, blessed be He; though He be high above all blessings and hymns, praises and consolations, which are uttered in the world; and say ye, Amen.'

'We must praise Him in adoration of His infinite wisdom, power and love. We must thank Him in gratitude for all the good things He lavishes on us. It is to Him that we must appeal for help and guidance in all our needs. In addition we must thank Him for any pleasure or good we enjoy in life, whether through food, drink, wonderful sights, or delightful odours.'[35]

Set times of prayer

The destruction of the first Temple, together with the experience of exile, seems to have led to a formalising of worship which perhaps did not previously exist. But 'by Daniel's time it seems ritual thrice daily prayer was established'.[36] There is a story of a man who asked Rabbi Judah the Prince why he did not pray every hour. 'It is forbidden,' said the Rabbi. Why? 'Because one ought not to treat the Almighty with frivolity.' This argument did not satisfy the enquirer, so the next day Rabbi Judah called on him every hour! 'Prayer should be at stated times–as an audience with an earthly king–"Evening, morning and noon-day" (Psalm 55:17).'[37]

In course of time, the Rabbis instituted the services of *Shacharith*, *Minchah* and *Ma'ariv* (morning, afternoon and evening). People may, of course, pray to God at any time; these are the times when it is mandatory to do so, both in the synagogue and the home. The times correspond to the times of the daily sacrifices in the Temple. Thus is reinforced the belief that prayer has taken the place of sacrifice. Among the morning prayers is one which surely inspired the poem at the beginning of this chapter: 'O my God, the soul which Thou gavest me is pure; Thou didst create it, Thou didst form it, Thou didst breathe it into me; Thou preservest it within me; and Thou wilt take it from me, but wilt restore it to me hereafter. So long as the soul is within me, I will give thanks unto Thee.'[38]

And from the night prayers we have: 'May it be Thy will, O Lord my God and God of my fathers, to suffer me to lie down in peace and to let me rise up again in peace. Let not my thoughts trouble me, nor evil dreams, nor evil fancies, but let my rest be perfect before Thee.'[39]

An essential part of the thrice daily prayers is the *Shemoneh Esreh*–the 'standing prayers' or *Amidah*. This consists of eighteen benedictions; it is considered the 'prayer par excellence' and so is designated by the term 'The *Tefillah*'. This incorporates the term 'a great God, a mighty and a terrible' (Deuteronomy 10:17), and concludes with the words, 'Let the words of my mouth and the meditation of my heart be acceptable before Thee, O Lord my Rock and my Redeemer' (Psalm 19:14).

Corporate prayer

Great value is put upon public, corporate prayers. They are less likely to be selfish. As Rabbi Isidore Epstein put it: 'Prayer, if recited at home, is liable to become merely a selfish thing. For this reason we have to try to join others in prayers as often as we can. The place best suited for this purpose is the synagogue.'[40] Rabbi Epstein went on to say that any place is acceptable to God. In the absence of a synagogue, Jewish people have been found praying together in all sorts of places–from the river-bank to the concentration camp! The place does not matter: 'It is not for the outside beauty of stones and bricks that God cares, but for the inner beauty of a prayerful heart.'

Participation in corporate prayers cements the sense of community. Judaism is a community religion, and public prayers are, to the Jew, 'his daily act of devotion as a unit in the body of Israel'.[41] Such prayers, it is believed, are especially pleasing to God. 'Let my prayer come before Thee at an acceptable time' (Psalm 69:13). 'When is that?' 'When the community prays.'[42] 'God says: If a man occupies himself with the Torah, practises benevolent acts, and prays with the congregation, I will ascribe it to him as though he had redeemed me and My son (Israel) from (exile) among the peoples of the world.'[43] Tradition has it that when ten men are praying in the house of God, the divine presence rests among them.[44] 'The prayer of an individual cannot be compared in worth to prayers offered by ten persons praying together.'[45] Hence it is that a congregation, to be valid, must number at least ten adult males (a *minyan*).

The elements of prayer

Various categories of prayer have been described. The *Zohar* lists thirteen, to correspond to the thirteen attributes of God.[46] Rabbi Samson Raphael Hirsch cites seven.[47] *The Jewish Encyclopedia* says: 'A tefillah consists of two parts: 1) Benedictions, or praises of God's greatness and goodness, and expressions of gratitude for benefits received; 2) Petitions, of either a public or a private nature.' Blessings–praises–are never omitted or glossed over:

> The Hallel (Psalm 113–118), that great paean of national and personal praise to God, is chanted equally as the worshippers' reassurance in times of trouble and distress. Not only an expression of thanks for God's benefits in the past, it prophetically thanks Him for all He is going to do in the future.
>
> Pain and suffering during the remaining uncertainties of life are bound to afflict in the years to come, yet affirmation of the all-and-always presence of God gives enabling power to journey fully strengthened through the depths of trouble and disaster, otherwise despair would take over and overwhelm.[48]

Petition may include confession as well as expressions of need, both temporal and spiritual. And, in whatever country a Jew finds himself, he is enjoined to 'Pray for the welfare of the government, for without it men would destroy each other alive.'[49]

No intermediary

Monotheism is the strongest tenet of Judaism. This has led to a conviction that there can be no intermediary between God and his people when they pray to him. If someone is sincere, and worthy, they will be heard, for 'every man in whom is the fear of God, his words are heard'.[50] It is true that the Kabbalists used to invoke *mal'ake rehamim* (angels of mercy). Their mysticism even bordered on the astrological. But that has always been seen by mainstream Judaism to be an aberration. To his people God says: 'If misfortune comes upon a man let him not cry to Michael, and not to Gabriel, but unto Me let him cry, and I will answer him right speedily, as it is said: Everyone who shall call upon the Name of the Lord shall be saved.'[51]

Toward Jerusalem

Daniel, in exile, is described as praying in his room which had windows opening toward Jerusalem (Daniel 6:10–11). Still today, world-wide, prayers are said facing toward Jerusalem. If one is in the land of Israel, one should turn toward the Temple site. 'Thus all Israel, at prayer, turn the face in the same direction.'[52] Some families have a plaque inscribed *Mizrach* in the home to indicate which direction is east. There is one on the window-sill of the room where I am writing. Always, in the heart of the Jewish people, is the longing for the land, the city and the Temple. This is their religion, their identity.

Attitudes of prayer

In ancient times, the Israelites prayed both kneeling and standing. Nowadays, perhaps partly as a reaction to the Christian custom of kneeling, prayers are said and sung standing. One should be humble in bearing; not, for instance, mounting a platform to pray in an exalted position, because 'Out of the depths I cry to you, O Lord' (Psalm 130:1). 'He shall direct his eyes downward and his heart upward.'[53] The higher one's rank, in worldly terms, the more important is this humble demeanour. There are certain places during the *Amidah* when it is customary to bow. The *Talmud* directs that 'the ordinary worshipper bows at the beginning and the end of the Amidah . . . The High Priest bows at every benediction; but the king remains kneeling until the end of the prayer, as did Solomon (1 Kings 8:54).'[54]

The outward signs of humility represent the inner attitude. Prayer is not to be undertaken casually. In ancient times the pious Rabbis would spend an hour in preparation for prayer, in obedience to the scripture: 'Prepare to meet your God, O Israel' (Amos 4:12). This preparation included the most scrupulous washing of the body.[55] The state of mind is all important. No one should pray with their mind in a turmoil: 'A man should always examine himself (before offering prayer); if he can direct his heart (to God), let him pray, otherwise he should not pray.'[56]

Prayer requires *kavannah*–concentration of mind, direction towards God, collectedness, calm. 'Kavannah in prayer is the basis of everything.'[57] It is necessary to acknowledge inwardly that one is approaching Almighty God, who created all that is, who gave *Torah* to his people, who merits their total allegiance and worship. 'Him do we recognise and to Him do we pray since everything is from Him.'[58] The highest form of prayer is offered with intensity and devotion–in fact, 'prayer without devotion is a body without a soul.'[59] The *Zohar* even says that 'prayer, when offered with intensity, is as flame to coal in uniting the higher and lower worlds.'[60]

One does not have to be learned in order to pray, nor is it necessary to come with skilful words. 'Even to the ignorant God says: Weep and pray, and I will receive you.'[61] But each should pray with all the abilities he has. Therefore some have taught that the sick should not pray, because they are not capable of concentration and *kavannah*. In such a case, they should just recite the *Shema* (Hear, O Israel . . . ': Deuteronomy 6:4–5).[62] The Chassidim believe that the important thing is for one's prayers to give pleasure to God–even 'petitionary prayer should be to please God in His role as Giver'.[63] The attitude is that being in a particular need gives an excuse for praying to God. 'What really matters for him is the joy of approaching his Maker.'[64]

Service of the heart

'In its highest sense it [tefillah] is the intimate communion between the creature and the Creator, deep speaking to deep.' True prayer is more than the utterance of the lips; it must come from the heart.[65] It is this kind of prayer which is known as 'the service of the heart'. 'What is meant by "to serve the Lord with all your heart" (Deuteronomy 11:13)?' asked the Rabbis. 'Surely this service of the heart is prayer.'[66] True prayer is service of the heart; true service of the heart is prayer. 'As long as Israel are looking upwards to their Father Who is in heaven they will live; if not, they will die.'[67] What Christians normally think of

as service is, in Rabbinic thought, inseparable from prayer.
Hirsch put it like this: 'The inner divine service [prayer]
should serve as a preparation of the outer one and should
realise, in it, its main purpose.'[68]

How is it possible, one may ask, to reconcile this teaching with the reality that so much of Judaism's prayer-life is
liturgical and formally prescribed? The answer, according
to the *Talmud*, is that one must use these forms to
enhance, not to limit, one's prayers. Thoughts may be
expressed in this way for which a man's own vocabulary
and imagination are insufficient. Certainly liturgy should
never be used as mere lip-service. 'This is true whether the
reference be to public or to private prayer. The inward
spirit must be the master and not the slave of whatever
outward form the prayer may assume.'[69] The Chassidim,
particularly, have placed great emphasis on this aspect of
prayer. Part of the message of the Baal Shem Tov[70] was:
'For the Creator, blessed be His Name, searches the heart
and knows all its secrets and it is the heart that He
wants.'[71] So contemplative prayer came to be one of
the hall-marks of Chassidism. 'In Chassidism prayer is
essentially an exercise in world-forsaking and abandon-
ment of self.'[72]

Spiritual renewal

The Rabbis have always taught that prayer is more than
petition and intercession, although it does include these
elements. The physical realm is real; material needs do
impinge. And God is concerned with these needs. But
more is to be looked for in prayer than the mere stating
and granting of requests. Prayer should actually achieve
something for the one praying, something beyond what is
usually thought of as 'answered prayer'. 'The Rabbis . . .

used prayer as the medium for enjoying fellowship with God and the development of what was purest and highest in human nature. The act of praying was their spiritual exercise for increasing the power of their soul to the end that it may become the dominant force in their life, the master of the flesh.'[73]

So the aim in prayer should be, not so much to change God's mind, as to be oneself changed. 'Prayer to God has . . . the salutary effect of purifying, refining, and ennobling our heart. It banishes evil thoughts, and thus saves us much pain and sorrow.'[74] Life has, historically, often been intolerable for Jewish people. Prayer has been one of the ways in which the Rabbis have sought to make the intolerable tolerable. Nothing may change outside, except for the worse, but we can be equipped with the means to survive and win through. One should strive in *tefillah* 'to renew your strength for life and regain your right and your will for truth, righteousness and love, as well as the power and the courage for victorious battle'.[75]

Prayer as submission

Jewish men are to pray daily wearing the *tefillin* (phylacteries)[76] upon the head and the upper arm, in literal obedience to Deuteronomy 11:18. The practice, as the Scriptures make clear, is to be symbolic.

> When a man puts on the head tefillin he makes his soul subordinate to God. When he puts on the hand tefillin he subordinates to God both his deeds and his heart . . . All man's thoughts and desires stem mainly from the heart, so that when he dons the hand tefillin man is reminded of his Maker . . . if, after donning the tefillin, man recites the Shema and then offers his prayers he has, indeed, taken upon himself

the yoke of the kingdom of heaven in the best manner possible.[77]

The *tallit* (prayer shawl, with fringes and tassels) is also worn for prayer, in accordance with Numbers 15:37–41.

A prayer from the *Talmud* may illustrate much of the best to be found in Jewish prayer:

> May it be Thy will, O Lord our God, to grant us long life, a life of peace, a life of good, a life of blessing, a life of sustenance, a life of bodily vigour, a life marked by the fear of sin, a life free from shame and reproach, a life of prosperity and honour, a life in which the love of Torah and the fear of heaven shall cleave to us, a life wherein Thou fulfillest all the desires of our heart for good.[78]

Jesus' prayer-life

For Jesus, prayer was an integral part of his humanity. He was in the habit of seeking God 'at the dawn' (Mark 1:35) and at other times (Matthew 14:23). There was no question, for him, of prayer taking the place of sacrifice–the Temple was still standing, the sacrifices still being offered. And he surely knew that he was himself destined to satisfy the sacrificial requirements (Matthew 20:28). We know that Jesus took part in Jewish religious life (Luke 4:16), and that he also prayed in specific circumstances: for the needs of others (John 11:41–43), and for himself–both in ministry and in his own hour of need (John 17:1–5).

We have what seems to be a full record of Jesus' prayer for the disciples which, in tune with the best of Jewish practice, expresses a yearning for their higher good: 'My prayer is not that you take them out of the world but that you protect them from the evil one . . . Sanctify them by the truth . . . that they may be one . . . that the love you have for me may be in them and that I myself may be in them' (John 17). Jesus prayed for them to *have* the best and *to be* the best for God.

There is no record that Jesus 'laid *tefillin*' (wore phylacteries) but neither do we know that he did not. Surely such a failure would have been cited against him by his many enemies. But he exemplified the submission symbolised in the practice when he prayed in Gethsemane: 'Father, if you are willing, take this cup from me; yet not my will, but yours be done' (Luke 22:42).

The 'Lord's Prayer'

The Jewish Encyclopedia points out that some of the phraseology of the pattern–prayer which Jesus taught his disciples was not new. *Avinu she-bashamayim* (Our Father who is in heaven); 'May his great name be extolled and hallowed'; 'May he establish his kingdom'; 'We will sanctify thy name in the world as they sanctify it in the highest heaven'; even 'Give us this day our daily bread'; all these expressions are to be found in Jewish prayers. It is certainly not true to say that God was not known as 'Father' before New Testament times. The pattern of praise before petition is familiar, but the connection between the giving and the receiving of forgiveness may have pulled the disciples up rather sharply–as it should ourselves today.

We saw that in his attitude to *Torah*, Jesus did not come to make righteousness easier, but to raise the standard. So it is with *tefillah*. The Hebrew Scriptures taught that a man should not approach God if someone had anything against him (Leviticus 6:1–7). Jesus built on that. He taught that we cannot really approach God if we ourselves are holding anything against another: 'Forgive us our sins, for we also forgive everyone who sins against us' (Luke 11:4).

But this is just a development of what was already Rabbinic practice. Is there anything radically new in Jesus' teaching about prayer, or was he just another Rabbi adding to the sum total of the collective tradition? The answer is to be found in John's Gospel, chapter 16, verses 23 and 24: 'I tell you the truth, my Father will give you whatever you ask in my name. Until now you have not asked for anything in my name. Ask and you will receive.'

As we have seen, Rabbinic tradition taught unequivocally that no intermediary was needed between man and God in prayer. The Rabbis based this doctrine on their belief in monotheism, but the Scriptures look to a different rationale–that of sacrifice. The first six chapters of Leviticus, laying down the various ritual sacrificial procedures, state repeatedly: 'The priest will make atonement . . . and he will be forgiven.' The relationship between the forgiver and the forgiven lies at the heart of prayer and, as Jesus himself was asked, 'Who can forgive sins but God alone?' (Mark 2:7). Jesus on that occasion declared that he had authority to forgive–claiming, in effect, equality with God–a claim backed up by the healing of the paralytic.

Surely the grounds upon which Jesus mediates between his disciples and God the Father in prayer is that of his sacrificial death. This is the bedrock difference between Jewish and Christian prayer. The Rabbis, since the destruction of the Temple, have had to formulate a system without sacrifice and, therefore, without mediation. Their solution has been: 'Tefillah (prayer), teshuvah (repentance), and tzedakah (charity) avert the evil decree.'

The New Testament teaches that there is a continuity between the Levitical sacrifices and the death of Jesus by which he procured for us, once for all, eternal redemption

(Hebrews 9:12). '[*Messiah*] was sacrificed once to take away the sins of many people' (Hebrews 9:28). It is because he is himself the sacrifice that he can mediate. It is because that sacrifice is eternally perfect that he is the *only* mediator. '[*Messiah*] Jesus, the [*Tzaddik*] (Righteous One) . . . is the atoning sacrifice for our sins, and not only for ours but also for the sins of the whole world' (1 John 2:1–2). Experience tells us that we can never achieve enough righteousness to be certain that our prayers will be accepted. Jesus achieved that righteousness on our behalf.

My husband was once asked: 'What is it, in one word, that you now have as a Jewish believer in Jesus which you did not have before?' Quick as a flash came the answer: 'Assurance.'

Notes

1 Samson Raphael Hirsch. Nineteenth-century German rabbi.
2 Samson Raphael Hirsch, *Horeb*, 1837 (Soncino Press, fourth edition, 1981), p.472.
3 Eric Lipson. Unpublished.
4 Rabbi Michael Friedlander, *The Jewish Religion*. (Shapiro, Vallentine and Co., 1922), p.183.
5 *A Rabbinic Anthology* (Macmillian and Co., Ltd., 1938), p.342.
6 *Midrash* on Psalm 5:4.
7 Ber.32b.
8 *Midrash* on Psalm 5:4.
9 *A Rabbinic Anthology*, p.346.
10 Rabbi Dr Louis Jacobs, *Hasidic Prayer* (Schocken Books, 1973), p.18.
11 Shab.10a.
12 Louis Jacobs, *op. cit*.
13 *The Jewish Encyclopedia* (Funk and Wagnalls Co., 1903).
14 Rabbi Michael Friedlander, *The Jewish Religion*, p.183.

15 *Ibid.*, p.185.
16 Dr J.H. Hertz, *A Book of Jewish Thoughts* (Oxford University Press, 1920), p.196.
17 William Mackintosh, *Gleanings from the Talmud* (Swan Sonnenschein, 1905), x:22.
18 Rev. Dr A. Cohen, *Everyman's Talmud* (J.M. Dent and Sons Ltd), pp.84, 87.
19 Yeb.64a.
20 *A Rabbinic Anthology*, p.344.
21 Rabbi Michael Friedlander, *op. cit.*, p.187.
22 *Ibid.*
23 *The Jewish Encyclopedia.*
24 Ber.29b.
25 *Siddur lev Chadash* (Union of Liberal and Progressive Synagogues, 1995), p.626.
26 Judah the Pious. Twelfth century.
27 Rabbi Michael Friedlander, *The Jewish Religion*, p.187.
28 Ber.12b.
29 Rev. Isidore Myers, *Gems from the Talmud* (Simpkin, Marshall, Hamilton, Kent and Co., 1894), para. 50.
30 *A Book of Jewish Thoughts*, p.237.
31 *A Rabbinic Anthology*, p.376.
32 Ber.29b.
33 *Ibid.*
34 *The Jewish Encyclopedia.*
35 Rabbi Dr Isidore Epstein, *Step By Step in the Jewish Religion* (Soncino Press, 1958), p.133.
36 *The Jewish Encyclopedia.*
37 Eric Lipson. Unpublished.
38 Ber.60b.
39 Ber.60b.
40 Rabbi Dr Isidore Epstein, *Step By Step in the Jewish Religion*, p.133.
41 Rev. Dr A. Cohen, trans., *Berakot* (Cambridge University Press, 1921), introduction, p.xxxi.
42 Ber.8a.

43 Rev. Dr A. Cohen, *Berakot.*
44 H. Polano, *The Talmud* (Frederick Warne and Co.), p.255.
45 Rabbi Dr Louis Jacobs, *Theology in the Responsa* (Routledge and Kegan Paul, 1975), p.55.
46 *The Jewish Encyclopedia.*
47 Samson Raphael Hirsch, *op. cit.*, p.478.
48 *The Jewish Encyclopedia.*
49 William Mackintosh, *op. cit.*, xlv:46.
50 Ber.6b.
51 William Mackintosh, *op. cit.*, xl:20.
52 Yer.Ber.4:5.
53 Yeb.105:5.
54 Yer.Ber.1:5.
55 Yer.Ber.3:4.
56 Ber.30b.
57 Rabbi Dr Louis Jacobs, *Theology in the Responsa* (Routledge and Kegan Paul, 1975), p.71.
58 *Ibid.*
59 William Mackintosh, *op. cit.*, x:2.
60 The *Zohar*, Wayakhel 213b.
61 *A Rabbinic Anthology*, p.343.
62 Rabbi Dr Louis Jacobs, *op. cit.*, p.35.
63 Rabbi Dr Louis Jacobs, *Hasidic Prayer*, p.30.
64 *Ibid.*, p.25.
65 Rev. Dr A. Cohen, *Everyman's Talmud*, p.87.
66 *A Rabbinic Anthology.*
67 William Mackintosh, *op. cit.*, x:19.
68 Samson Raphael Hirsch, *op. cit.*, p.471.
69 Ber.18b.
70 Israel ben Eliezer. c. 1700–60. The founder of Chassidism.
71 Rabbi Dr Louis Jacobs, *op. cit.*, p.34.
72 *Ibid.*, p.21.
73 Rev. Dr A. Cohen, *Everyman's Tlamud*, p.93.
74 Rabbi Michael Friedlander, *op. cit.*, p.183.
75 Samson Raphael Hirsch, *op. cit.*, pp.472–473.

76 Leather boxes bound on the forehead and the arm during prayer, containing four passages (Exodus 13:1–10; 11–16; Deuteronomy 6:4–9; 13–21) on parchment.

77 Rabbi Dr Louis Jacobs, *Theology in the Responda*, p.134.

78 Ber.16b.

צְדָקָה

My husband used to tell this story against himself. In the days when he was warden of a Jewish settlement in East London, it was quite common for him to be approached by needy people–*schnorrers* (beggars). Times were hard, poverty widespread. Many were in genuine need and would spend the money wisely–perhaps to get essential tools out of pawn; some would be feckless and throw it away on drink. How was one to know? One day he rebuked a man who seemed to be constantly on the scrounge; why couldn't he pull himself together, get some sort of job, take responsibility for himself and his family?

'Who are you to pass judgement on me, you who are more fortunate than I? Your duty is to dispense charity to the needy.'

Eric accepted the rebuke, and never forgot it. The man was right. In Judaism, one of the highest forms of virtue is charity, closely associated with righteousness–*Tzedakah*.

10

TZEDAKAH

צְדָקָה

Mitzvah

'The word mitzvah (literally 'commandment') sums up all that is both right and kindly in Jewish practice. It has come to mean not merely that which is mandatory, laid down by law, or the carrying out of some religious observance, but the good deed, an act of thoughtfulness, anything done by one person that helps or makes more pleasant the life of another; in short, any good thing involving heart, mind and action.'[1] In common parlance, one speaks of the performance of a kindness as 'it's a *mitzvah*'.

There are two categories of charity: 1) *Tzedakah* (almsgiving, literally 'righteousness'); 2) *Gemiluth chasadim* (the bestowal of loving acts, benevolence). According to *Everyman's Talmud*, the use of *tzedakah* to mean 'almsgiving' goes back, 'possibly to Daniel (4:27), certainly to Ecclesiasticus (3:14 and 7:10)'.[2]

Righteousness

'Charity is righteousness.'[3] In Hebrew thought it gives
the sense of doing *right* by a person. This is not the same
as the commonly accepted meaning of the word, which is
derived from the Greek word *charis*–an undeserved gift–
something condescendingly given from my bounty to
your poverty. Job drew on the Hebrew idea when he
claimed, in his defence, 'I put on righteousness as my
clothing . . . I was eyes to the blind and feet to the lame.
I was a father to the needy' (29:15–16). This is the
epitome of the righteous man. 'Nothing is more marked
in Rabbinic ethics than the stress laid upon charity in
every sense of the word–from almsgiving to all sorts of
lovingkindness.'[4] Righteousness is equated with social
justice by Amos (5:7) and Daniel (4:27). And in the
twentieth century Epstein,[5] echoing an ancient Rabbinic
dictum, has written: 'Righteousness teaches that we
should do unto others what we would like to have
done to ourselves.'[6] So it can be seen that there is a
blurring of the dividing line between *tzedakah* and *gemiluth chasadim*.

Gemiluth chasadim (benevolence)

The prophet Isaiah taught that one should spend oneself
(literally 'draw out one's soul') on behalf of the needy
(58:10). This is interpreted to mean that even if one has
nothing material to give, one must offer one's self–true
heartfelt sympathy. This kind of charity is, according to
Dr Cohen, 'superior in ethical quality and of greater value
to mankind' even than almsgiving.[7] The *Talmud* goes so
far as to claim that '*Gemiluth Chasadim* is one of the three
pillars upon which the world (ie the social order) rests'.[8] It

is greater than almsgiving in three respects: 1) Almsgiving is performed with money–benevolence with either personal service or money; 2) Almsgiving is restricted to the poor–benevolence can be displayed to both poor and rich; 3) Almsgiving can only be done to the living–benevolence to both the living and the dead.[9]

The Chassidic Anthology records the Braztlaver[10] as saying: 'He who gives a penny to a poor man receives six blessings; he who shows his sympathy with the poor man receives eleven blessings.'[11] And the supreme importance of benevolence is reinforced by this Talmudic comment: 'The Pentateuch begins with an act of benevolence and concludes with an act of benevolence. At the beginning it is said, "And the Lord God made for Adam and his wife coats of skins and clothed them" (Genesis 3:21); and at the end it is said, "And He buried him [Moses] in the valley" (Deuteronomy 34:6).'[12]

Categories of charity

Josephus[13] recorded that charity, according to Moses, was 'to afford fire, water and food to such as need them, to show them the road and not to let anyone lie unburied'.[14] This basic teaching has been elaborated over the centuries. The Chassidim[15] are said to have practised seven branches of charitable work:[16]

1) Feeding the hungry and giving the thirsty drink;
2) Clothing the naked;
3) Visiting the sick;
4) Burying the dead and comforting the mourners;
5) Redeeming the captive;
6) Educating the fatherless and sheltering the homeless;
7) Providing poor maidens with dowries.

The *Talmud* elaborates even further. A people driven so often to wander from one persecution to another have needed to know that hospitality is assured at the end of the journey–particularly Sabbath hospitality–hence: 'Greater is the reception of wayfarers than the reception of the Shechinah.'[17] And the importance of sick-visiting has been underlined: 'Whoever visits the sick takes away a sixtieth part of his illness–so let sixty people visit him and set him on his feet again.'[18] Indeed, the importance of this particular *mitzvah* is underlined by Rabbi Akiba[19] who said, 'Whoever does not visit the sick is as though he sheds blood.'[20] *A Rabbinic Anthology* also specifies the duty of helping widows and orphans.

Epstein reduces the list to four:

1) Giving money to the begging poor;
2) Feeding the hungry;
3) Clothing the naked;
4) Giving hospitality to the wayfarer.[21]

Jesus of Nazareth was well within the heart of this teaching when he told the parable of the sheep and the goats (Matthew 25:31–46): 'I was hungry and you gave me something to eat, I was thirsty and you gave me something to drink, I was a stranger and you invited me in, I needed clothes and you clothed me, I was sick and you looked after me, I was in prison and you came to visit me . . . whatever you did for one of the least of these brothers of mine, you did for me.'

The highest form of *tzedakah* is traditionally that of ministry to the dead, because this is the only good deed for which there can be no hope of recompense, and is therefore performed from wholly pure motives. Assistance at a funeral is regarded as of sacred importance–even 'the study of Torah may be interrupted to bear out a corpse and to help a bride to marry.'[22] Alongside this is the duty of comforting the mourners, said to be one of the deeds by which man may imitate God himself. But comfort should not be untimely or insensitively offered; 'Comfort not your fellow man in the hour when his dead lies before him;'[23] it is inappropriate to offer words of consolation in the hours immediately after bereavement. Mourners should be visited during the seven days of mourning which follow the funeral.

Degrees of charity

Maimonides[24] enumerates eight ranks of those who give charity:

1) He who aids the poor man in supporting himself by advancing money or helping him to some lucrative occupation;
2) He who gives charity without knowing who is the recipient, and without the recipient knowing who is the giver;
3) He who gives in secret, casting the money into the houses of the poor, who remain ignorant as to their benefactor;
4) He who gives without knowing the recipient, by casting it among the poor, while the recipient knows who is the giver;
5) He who gives before he is asked;
6) He who gives after he is asked;
7) He who gives inadequately, but with a good grace;
8) He who gives with a bad grace.

It is generally recognised that the highest form of charity is that which strengthens the hand of the recipient so that he no longer needs to be an object of charity; and the lowest form is that which is given grudgingly and ungraciously. This is consistent with *Talmudic* tradition, which says: 'Of greater merit than giving is the helping of the poor by lending him money, or in some other way facilitating his mode of living.'[25] This view is based on the Mosaic teaching of Leviticus 25:35.

Jesus recognised this highest form of *tzedakah* when he faced the blind man with the question, 'What do you want me to do for you?' (Luke 18:41). To most people, the man's need was obvious. He was a beggar; he needed money. But Jesus was able to put him in a position where he no longer needed to beg–he could stand on his own feet. Was that what he really wanted, or did he prefer a life of dependence? The Rabbi from Nazareth gave him his sight, his independence and his dignity–a true act of *tzedakah*.

Perhaps Peter and John had this in mind when the lame man asked them for alms (Acts 3:1–10). What they gave him, in the name of Jesus the Messiah of Nazareth was so much better than alms–strengthening 'the hand of the recipient so that he no longer needed to be an object of charity'.

The Rabbis have always held that a state of social misery is unacceptable. When the kingdom of God/ Messianic kingdom comes, these wrongs will be abolished. But, in the meantime, they have never been content with simply feeding the poor. Their great ideal was not to allow anyone to be poor, not to allow them to come down into the depths of poverty. One should teach the poor person a trade–indeed trying all methods before permitting them to become an object of charity and so be degraded.

Chief Rabbi Sacks,[26] commenting on Maimonides, dares to draw this teaching to a more radical conclusion:

Nothing more clearly defines the place of charity in the system than this: it may be the highest virtue, but better is the world where it is not needed. Charity is not justified by the good it does to the soul of the giver, but by the degree to which it removes the misery of the recipient . . . an act which enables him not to need charity is higher than any charity.'[27]

Dr Sacks is reflecting a late twentieth-century worldview which would have been unthinkable to the ancients–that the ideal for which to aim, and which ought to be achievable, is a society in which charity is not needed. The Bible is more realistic: 'There will always be poor people in the land' (Deuteronomy 15:11); as was Jesus: 'The poor you will always have with you' (Matthew 26:11).

How charity should be given

Four 'dispositions' of almsgivers are described in the *Talmud*:[28]

1) He who desires to give but that others should not give, his eye is evil towards what appertains to others;
2) He who desires that others should give but will not give himself, his eye is evil against what is his own;
3) He who gives and wishes others to give is a saint;
4) He who will not give and does not wish others to give is a wicked man.

Here we begin to see that not the gift alone, but also the motive which lies behind it, is weighed in the balance. Am I primarily concerned with the well-being of the needy, or with my own 'brownie points'? And how considerate am I of the dignity and 'face' of my fellow man or woman? One should never give charity in such a manner as to shame the recipient; it is even said, 'Better give him nothing than put him to shame.'[29] The highest praise is for the one who gives in secret: 'Greater than Moses is he who gives charity anonymously.'[30] What higher praise can there be than that?

'Be careful not to do your "acts of righteousness" before men,' taught Jesus. 'When you give to the needy, do not annnounce it with trumpets . . . when you give to the needy, do not let your left hand know what your right hand is doing, so that your giving may be in secret' (Matthew 6:1–4).

Deeper than what is shown is what is thought and felt. The charity must be given out of a heart of love and in a loving manner: 'Almsgiving becomes increasingly perfect according to the amount of love that is shown in it.'[31] The recipient is not to be thought of as an inferior being, and is certainly never to be treated with lack of consideration or with contempt.

According to biblical precept, the gift should always be appropriate to the need: 'If there is a poor man among your brothers . . . do not be hard-hearted or tight-fisted towards your poor brother. Rather be open-handed and freely lend him whatever he needs' (Deuteronomy 15:7–8). Moreover, the ancient Israelites were not to be influenced in their generosity by thoughts of the nearness of the year of Jubilee, when debts would be rescinded (v.9). The *Talmud* comments on Deuteronomy 15:11 ('I command you to be open-handed towards your brothers and towards the poor and needy in the land'): 'To him for whom bread is suitable, give bread; to him who needs dough, give dough; to him for whom money is required, give money; to him for whom it is fitting to put food in his mouth, put it in.'[32] And on Psalm 41:1 ('Blessed is he who has regard for the weak') the injunction is: 'It is not written, "Happy is he who *gives* to the poor", but "Happy is he who *considers* the poor."'[33] This means considering his dignity and also his previous estate; the standard of living to which he is accustomed is to be taken into account.

The importance of charity

A very high value indeed is placed upon the *mitzvah* of charity. Simon the Just[34] went so far as to say, 'Upon three things the world is based: upon the Torah, upon the Temple service, and upon the doing of loving deeds [*gemiluth chasadim*].'[35] This is a tradition that has been honoured through the ages; Epstein rated it even above the observance of *Shabbat*: 'It is our duty, when we see a human being in peril or distress, to come to his rescue and to do everything in our power to save him. This duty overrides all other commandments of our Torah. Even the Sabbath must be broken, if necessary, in order to help a man in danger.'[36] And the Bratzlaver taught that one should give charity before commencing one's prayers–that way alien thoughts would be avoided.

In his arrangement *The Book of Jewish Thoughts*, Chief Rabbi Dr Hertz[37] gave one explanation for the importance of charity

> The dispensing of charity according to one's means is a positive precept, which demands greater care and diligence in its performance than all the other positive precepts of the Law. For its neglect may possibly lead to the taking of life, inasmuch as the denial of timely aid may compass the death of the poor man who needs our immediate help.

Dr Hertz cites Isaiah 54:14 ('In righteousness you will be established') as authority for his statement that 'Charity is the main foundation of Israel's pre-eminence, and the basis of the Law of Truth'. The Chassidim, too, rated charity highly. The Bratzlaver is quoted as saying, 'Charity has the weight of all the mitzvoth together,' and, 'Charity is of great use on the Judgment Day.'[38]

A Rabbinic Anthology notes that Proverbs 10:2 ('Tzedakah [righteousness, charity] delivers from death') was taken very seriously by the Rabbis, who interpreted 'death' in this case as meaning 'hell', or long residence in purgatory, or even total deprivation of eternal bliss in the hereafter. Rather than risk depriving the supplicant of what they need, one should be prepared to give to the 'con man'; better to be deceived than to be guilty of refusing the needy. Hence my husband's acceptance of the *schnorrer's* rebuke. Lack of *tzedakah* was even given as the reason for Israel's open-ended exile from the land: 'Twice did Israel go into exile: for the first time, a time of return was given, but for the second, none. Why? Though the men of the first Temple practised idolatry, yet there was proper behaviour (derek eretz) among them. And what was this 'derek eretz'? Almsgiving and deeds of loving-kindness.'[39]

And, of course, the ideal type of the virtuous woman is the one praised every *Shabbat* eve by her husband as she who not only 'watches over the affairs of her household' (Proverbs 31:27) but also 'opens her arms to the poor and extends her hands to the needy' (Proverbs 31:20).

Tzedakah was not only a private, individual matter. Every community would customarily have a charity box so that the poor, both local and transient, could be given immediate support. In passing, it is interesting that Epstein points out that *tzedakah* was not only to be practised towards human beings. 'Righteousness, as a standard of conduct . . . includes all living creatures, animals no less than human beings' and 'is also concerned with the rest of creation, besides human beings and animals.'[40]

Tzedakah brings blessing

Everyone has a duty to practise *tzedakah*: 'Even the poor man who is living on tzedakah shall give tzedakah from what he can spare from his upkeep.'[41] This is because of the blessing it confers on the giver, as well as the receiver. This thought is brought out in Israel Zangwill's delightful book *The King of Schnorrers*. The *schnorrer* (beggar) points out to the wealthy that he is needed to enable them to satisfy the requirements of religion; hence, he reasons, it could be said that the poor man does more for the rich man than the rich does for the poor! 'Why does God not provide for the poor?' asked Rabbi Akiba. 'So that through them we may be delivered from the penalty of gehinnon.'

Akiba saw the benefits as being more universal than that: 'God, the Father of both the rich and the poor, wants the one to help the other, and thus make the world a household of love.' 'Charity in its various branches, tzedakah and gemiluth chasadim, is a virtue practised by the wealthy and the poor alike. Any heart or house from which this virtue is absent does not deserve to be called Jewish.'[42]

The benefits are various. Just as the absence of *tzedakah* caused the *Shechinah* to depart, so does its practice cause *Shechinah* to approach.[43] Even good health was promised, according to a proverb: 'The door which is not open to charity is open to the doctor.'[44] The blessings are psychological too; there will be the 'supreme happiness of giving, the bliss of the knowledge that you have fed the hungry, clothed the naked, comforted the sick, cheered the unhappy, provided for the needy'. And, over and above all this, said Hirsch, 'You will rejoice in the great task to which God has called you–to be a blessing with all that you possess.'[45]

The absence of *tzedakah*, by contrast, draws harsh judgement. It has even been equated with idolatry. Only a worthless man will harden his heart against the needy. This is in the biblical tradition of the prophets. Amos had harsh words for those who practised the externals of religion but neglected compassion to the needy. He accused Israel of turning moral standards upside down: 'You who turn justice into bitterness and cast righteousness to the ground' (5:7). He saw the poor and vulnerable being victimised and trampled upon and issued a challenge that would be appropriate for our own generation and society: 'Let justice roll on like a river, righteousness like a never-failing stream' (5:24). Isaiah yearned for the coming of the kingdom, but knew that even the best of God's people would be found wanting before God's aweful holiness: 'All our righteous acts are like filthy rags,' he acknowledged (64:6).

Jesus, too, was scathing about this particular form of hypocrisy: 'Woe to you, Pharisees, because you give God a tenth of your mint, rue and all other kinds of garden herbs, but you neglect justice and the love of God' (Luke 11:42). Our possessions, it is taught, are not our own in perpetuity. So we are not entitled to hold them only for our own benefit and pleasure. Epstein has taught that this belief was the basis for the Jewish teaching on *tzedakah*.[46] Man must know that he is not the master of his possessions, but only the guardian. His duty is to carry out the will of God–who trusted these things to him in the first place. This follows the thinking of King David: 'Everything comes from you, and we have given you only what comes from your hand' (1 Chronicles 29:14). Jesus underlined this idea of responsibility and the response of gratitude: 'Your Father has been pleased to give you the kingdom. Sell your possessions and give to the poor' (Luke 12:32–33).

Tzedakah and atonement

Hosea's words, 'I desire mercy, not sacrifice' (6:6) have led the Rabbis to see *tzedakah* as being effective for atonement. Indeed, it has been regarded as a form of sacrifice offered to God.[47] The thinking is that God has no need to eat, so giving food to the poor is accepted by him instead of sacrifices. 'Almsgiving is greater than all sacrifices, for it says, "To give alms, [literally 'to do justice'] is more acceptable to God than sacrifices" (Proverbs 21:3)'.[48] It is a short step from here to believe that *tzedakah*, together with *teshuvah* and *tefillah*, 'avert the evil decree' in the absence of the Temple and, therefore, of sacrifices.

But this is not to be a facile way of fulfilling the requirements of *Yom Kippur* (the Day of Atonement). Just as only the best–perfect, unblemished–animals were acceptable for sacrifice so, said Hirsch, 'Do you wish genuinely to fulfil the duty of *tzedakah*? Then let it be the best of your possessions that you sacrifice, the best food to the hungry, the best raiment to the naked; for it is a sacrifice laid upon God's altar–let it be a worthy sacrifice.'[49] And the Bratzlaver developed the thought of one aspect of atonement when he said, 'Charity and kind deeds are the best mediators between Israel and their Father in heaven.'[50] Not only does *tzedakah* mediate between Israel and God; it is also said to bring nearer 'the redemption'–the coming of Messiah, as a fulfilment of Isaiah 1:27: 'Zion will be redeemed with justice, her penitent ones with righteousness'.

Tzedakah alone will not achieve atonement and forgiveness. There has to be repentance (*teshuvah*) as well. In fact, Rabbi Apple wrote that:

Tzedakah–which means 'righteous action' in the widest sense–is the proof that our repentance is sincere, and therefore teshuvah must be accompanied by an improvement in one's deeds. We read in the book of Jonah on Yom Kippur afternoon that only when God saw the deeds of the people of Nineveh did He know for certain that they had really repented.[51]

James talked about the connection between *tzedakah* and inner change. 'Suppose a brother or sister is without clothes and daily food. If one of you says to him, "Go, I wish you well; keep warm and well fed," but does nothing about his physical needs, what good is it?' (2:15–16). Charity, he is saying, arises out of change, described here as 'faith'. How can faith be considered genuine if it does not issue in *tzedakah*?

The story of Cornelius (Acts 10) is interesting. The man's sincerity was measured by his acts of charity, but still something was lacking. Peter was sent to show him the way to fill his greatest lack. He needed to find forgiveness–yes, even this good, God-fearing man–through faith in Jesus the Messiah, Lord of all. To the Messianic Jew/Christian, charity is highly estimable, but as the outworking and sign of faith in the atoning Messiah–not as itself the means of atonement.

Notes

1 Eric Lipson. Unpublished.
2 Rev. Dr A. Cohen, *Everyman's Talmud* (J.M. Dent and Sons Ltd., reprint 1937), p.233.
3 *The Jewish Encyclopedia* (Funk and Wagnalls Co., 1903).
4 *A Rabbinic Anthology* (Macmillan and Co. Ltd, 1938), p.412.
5 Rabbi Dr Isidore Epstein. Principal Jews' College, London, the middle years of the twentieth century.

6 Rabbi Dr Isidore Epstein, *Step By Step in the Jewish Religion* (Soncino Press, 1958), p.34.
7 Rev. Dr A Cohen, *op. cit.*, p.238.
8 Avoth 1:2.
9 Suk.49:b.
10 Rabbi Nachman of Bratzlav. 1770-1811.
11 Louis I. Newman, *The Chassidic Anthology* (Charles Scribner's Sons, 1934), p.41.
12 Sot.14:a.
13 Roman general and historian. First century.
14 *Contra Ap.* 2:29.
15 A sect founded in the eighteenth century by Rabbi Israel ben Eliezer (the 'Besht' or 'Baal Shem Tov'). Sought to experience the love of God and serve him with enthusiam and joy.
16 *The Jewish Encyclopedia.*
17 Shabb.127a.
18 Ned.39:b.
19 Akiba ben Joseph. First century. Sometimes called 'the father of Rabbinical Judiasm'.
20 Ned.40:a.
21 Rabbi Dr Isidore Epstein, *op. cit.*, p.39.
22 Meg.3:b.
23 Avoth 4:23.
24 Moses ben Maimon (RaMBaM). Thirteenth-century *Talmudist*, philosopher, astronomer, physician. Born Spain. Died Egypt.
25 Shab.63:a.
26 Rabbi Dr Jonathan Sacks. Chief Rabbi of the United Hebrew Congregations of the British Commonwealth.
27 Rabbi Dr Jonathan Sacks, *Tradition in an Untraditional Age* (Vallentine, Mitchell, 1990), p.186.
28 Avoth 5:16.
29 Chag.5:a.
30 The Bratzlaver.
31 Suk.49:b.

32 Sifre Deuteronomy.
33 T.J. Pe'ah 8:9.
34 Identity uncertain. High Priest either third or second century BC.
35 Montefiore and Loewe, *op. cit.*, p.430.
36 Rabbi Dr Isidore Epstein, *op.cit.*, p.35.
37 Chief Rabbi of Great Britain in the early years of this century.
38 Louis I. Newman *op. cit.*, pp.40–41.
39 Montefiore and Loewe, *op. cit.*, p.416.
40 Rabbi Dr Isidore Epstein, *op. cit.*, pp.43,46.
41 Samson Raphael Hirsch, *Horeb* 1837 (Soncino Press, fourth edition, 1981), p.429.
42 Rabbi Michael Friedlander, *The Jewish Religion* (Shapiro, Vallentine and Co., 1922), pp.469–470.
43 The Bratzlaver.
44 Pes.R.42:b.
45 Samson Raphael Hirsch, *op. cit.*, pp.427–428.
46 Rabbi Dr Isidore Epstein, *op. cit.*, p. 88.
47 *The Jewish Encyclopedia.*
48 Suk.49:b.
49 Samson Raphael Hirsch, *op. cit.*, p.429.
50 Louis I. Newman, *op. cit.*, p.40.
51 Raymond Apple, *Companion to the Machzor for Rosh Hashanah and Yom Kippur* (United Synagogue Publications Committee, 1964), p.27.

הושיענא

Whatever could be happening? All those people streaming out towards the Jericho road. This time of year, just before Passover, was when folk moved into Jerusalem–not away from it.

'What's going on?'

'They say there's a man riding into Jerusalem on a donkey.'

'So what; that's nothing special.'

'They say it's that rabbi from Galilee.'

'People are throwing garments and palm branches in his path. They're going wild out there!'

'They say it's what the prophet said would happen.'

'Listen, you can hear what they're shouting: *Hosha'na*! *Hosha'na* to the Son of David!'

'But that means . . . O surely not!'

'And yet–could it be? Could he be the one of whom the prophet spoke?'

'You can't mean . . . is it possible?'

'Who is this man? Who *is* he?'

11

HOSHA'NA

הוֹשִׁיעָֽנָא

'*Hoshi'ah-na*'–'O Lord, save us!' is a cry traditionally associated with *Succoth* (the Feast of Tabernacles), though the familiar Palm Sunday story is set, of course, in the days leading up to *Pesach* (Passover). Usually abbreviated, 'probably owing to constant repetition',[1] to '*Hosha'na*', this cry of 'Help!' from the Jewish people has not, historically, been confined to any one season.

Succoth

Succoth, 'the Festival of our Rejoicing', is the culmination of the Jewish year, symbolising all there is to hope for in the future. 'Like threads of gold across the tapestry of the Jewish year run the nine days of Succoth,' wrote Rabbi Lehrman in the dark days of 1943.[2] This is the last of the festivals ordained in Leviticus 23, following closely on *Rosh Hashanah* (New Year/the Festival of Trumpets) and *Yom Kippur* (the Day of Atonement). It is the Harvest Festival of the Ingathering, as well as a reminder of God's care for Israel when they dwelt in *succoth* (booths) during the forty years of their desert wanderings.

In the home it is customary to build a *succah*, a temporary, outdoor structure through which the stars can be seen, decorated with branches and fruit, in which to praise God for that past protection. During each of the the first six days, worshippers process once round the synagogue, each holding the 'four species'–the *Lulav* and the *Ethrog*. The *Ethrog* is a citron–a lemon-like fruit 'which is both pleasant in appearance and fragrance, and typifies a life of fruitful activity'.

The *Lulav* is made up of a palm branch together with willow and myrtle bound together. 'The willow, which lacks both beauty and fragrance, withering easily and yielding no fruit, portrays the useless and selfish life.' 'The myrtle, which though comely in appearance is not fruit-bearing, reminds one of the godly life that lives for itself alone.' 'The palm is the most ideal of plants. Stately in height and bearing fruit even in the desert, it stands for the life of dignity and goodwill, ever ready to share its blessings with others.' Thus, there is represented here the sum total of Jewry–the good and the bad. The binding together of these 'four species' is said to symbolise the importance of unity in the Jewish community.[3] The waving of the *Lulav* in all directions is also thought to symbolise the omnipresence of God.

In Temple times, libations of water were made on the intermediate days of *Succoth* and, still today, rain is prayed for. After all, the harvest may have been gathered in–but how will one eat next year unless the rain falls soon, to soften the ground for ploughing? This water ceremony was performed amid great rejoicing. 'Whence do we know that great jubilation used to take place at the water-libation?–because it says (Isaiah 12:3): "And ye shall draw water in joy."'[4] 'He who has not seen the joy at the water-libation has never seen joy in his life.'[5] It is probable that Jesus was referring to this ceremony when, in the Temple courts during *Succoth*, he 'stood and said in a loud voice, "If anyone is thirsty, let him come to me and drink"' (John 7:37–38).

Hosha'na Rabbah

'The joyousness of the Feast of Booths, as it gathered around the "drawing of water" and developed in music and torchlight processions, attained its height on the seventh day.'[6] The popular name for this day is *Hosha'na Rabbah*–'the Great *Hosha'na*'. It is a point of climax in the festival, and marks a change of mood. Instead of one circuit of the synagogue there are seven, accompanied by many prayers for salvation (*Hoshi'a-na*)–hence the name traditionally associated with the day.

On the previous days one or, at the most, two scrolls of *Torah* (the 'Law') are carried in procession as the men say, '*Hoshi'a-na*! for thy sake, our God! *Hoshi'a-na*! For thy sake, our creator! For thy sake, our redeemer, *Hoshi'a-na*!' On this day, all the scrolls are carried on the seven circuits. On each circuit a different prayer is said, with the repeated chorus, '*Hoshi'a-nna*!' ('O save now, we beseech thee') reminding God of his mercies in the past and his people's great need today. For instance, this is the prayer on the third circuit:

Moses delivered her once–the sanctified sheep of his fold
Were Jacob's assembly of old
Marked by Thy Name: O save!
They are falling, they grasp Thee, they crave,
They are calling, beseeching Thee, 'Save!'[7]

From as early as the Hasmonean period[8] the character of this particular day developed into something much more solemn than that of the preceding days of the festival. The constant repetition of the cry, '*Hoshi'a-na*' does not sit well with jollity. This trend was intensified by the Chassidic movement:

> Towards the end of the Middle Ages, with the rise of mysticism, the seventh day–*Hosha'na Rabbah*–grew greatly in solemnity. By the sixteenth century, the day came to be looked upon as a continuation of the Day of Atonement, giving 'another chance' for repentance to those sinful mortals who had on that Holy Day failed to make full use of the Divine grace.[9]

'According to tradition, God waits until this day for the sinner to return. The plaintive melodies of Yom Kippur are reintroduced and the Reader once again dons his white "kittel"[10].'[11] So the belief is that a person's fate, forgiven or not, is finally decided on this day. No wonder that in many communities it has been customary for the more devout to spend the preceding night in vigil, reciting the prayers of repentance for *Hosha'na Rabbah*.[12] 'The main idea of the day,' said Rabbi Lehrman, 'was to point out to the Jew that it is never too late to repent.'[13] And so, on the seventh circuit, in addition to the enumeration of God's past deliverances, there is the theme of forgiveness associated with that of salvation:

> O God! Like sheep we all have gone astray;
> from out Thy Book wipe not our name away.
> Save! Save!
> I beseech Thee, O God, save! O save, I beseech Thee.
>   Thou art our Father.[14]

As a sign of repentance, after the seventh circuit the *Lulav* and *Ethrog* are laid aside and bundles of willow (*Hoshanot*) taken up. It is said that in Temple times willow branches about fourteen feet long were set up, for the occasion, at the sides of the altar, with their branches overhanging it. Towards the end of the service, these are struck repeatedly until the leaves fall off, 'accompanied by an eloquent prayer that our sins be cast off as the leaves which now strew the synagogue;'[15] 'O God, save, yea save, we beseech Thee. O save, O forgive, O send prosperity; yea save us, God of our stronghold.'[16]

There is a further interpretation of the use of the willows and the accompanying prayers. A hint of it is found in the liturgy: 'A man hath sprung forth, and the Branch his name is–/yea, David himself, 'tis King David, rejoice!'[17]

The willows express the hope of resurrection and of the Messianic age. The leafless trees in the autumn, symbolised by the beaten willows, resume new life and produce fresh flowers and fruits after being visited by the rain and dew of the spring. This symbolises the end of one season and the beginning of another. So will the lifeless body be restored to everlasting life 'in the end of days'.[18]

Save, we beseech thee

There are several Hebrew words which relate to *Hosha'na*. The primitive meaning of *yasha* is 'to be or to make wide'. 'Evil and danger are always regarded as narrowing conditions or effects.' So the Psalmist (Psalm 118:5) cries out to God from his 'narrow' place. When help comes he will be in a 'wide' place.[19] Salvation is therefore the opposite of every form of constriction or enslavement. So the word came to mean 'to save'. The day that God brought Israel through the Red Sea or sea of Reeds in safety they were 'saved'–delivered (Exodus 14:30). Likewise Israel was assured that when they would go forth to battle in their own land, to the sound of the silver trumpets, God would remember them and 'save'–rescue–them (Numbers 10:9).

Yesha means 'safety'–'salvation'. 'Restore to me the joy of your salvation)' cried David in repentance (Psalm 51:12), feeling that, by his sin, he had placed himself outside the 'safety zone' of God's enfolding arms. And Habakkuk, in his reassurance of a faith so deeply questioned, knew that, no matter what disasters struck, he would be able to rejoice in the God of his salvation (Habakkuk 3:18).

Similarly, *yeshua* means 'breadth', 'ease', 'safety', 'salvation.' 'Stand firm,' said Moses on the Egyptian side of the Sea, 'and you will see the [salvation] (deliverance) the Lord will bring you today' (Exodus 14:13). 'Surely God is my salvation' will be Israel's song one day (Isaiah 12:2). They will then be at ease, in safety, able to trust and not be afraid. Then they will indeed 'draw water from the wells of salvation' (Isaiah 12:3). This kind of safety can only come in the Messianic age. 'In that day' is Isaiah's refrain: 'In that day they will say, surely this is our God; we trusted in him, and he saved us . . . let us rejoice and be glad in his salvation' (Isaiah 25:9).

Nosha means, primarily, 'the recipient of salvation'. Zechariah saw the coming king as 'righteous and having salvation' (Zechariah 9:9). He would have salvation because he had received it, but also he would have it to offer. That is why his coming would be a cause for rejoicing.

Zechariah 9:9

> Rejoice greatly, O Daughter of Zion!
> Shout, Daughter of Jerusalem!
> See, your king comes to you,

righteous and having salvation,
gentle and riding on a donkey,
on a colt, the foal of a donkey.

Jewish tradition has always seen this prophecy as being
connected to the national regathering. Salvation is interpreted in those terms. Although Ibn Ezra[20] believed it to
be an allusion to Judas Maccabeus,[21] the majority view
has been that of Kimchi:[22] 'The writings of the Jews
furnish an unbroken chain of testimony to prove that it
[Zechariah 9:9] always referred to the Messiah.'[23] This
verse even became a sort of litmus test for every pretender
to the Messiahship.[24] Rashi[25] said, 'This can only refer to
King Messiah of whom it is said: "And his dominion shall
be from sea to sea", since we do not find any ruler with
such wide dominion during the days of the second
Temple.'[26]

This Messiah will come bringing both God's judgement
and his salvation. The primary target for this coming will
be Israel, God's 'splendour' (Isaiah 46:13); Israel is where
God's kingdom, one of salvation, will be established.[27]
But the view is not solely national. Israel is intended to
mediate God's final salvation to all. 'The consummation of
our and mankind's salvation will take place in Messianic
times'[28] said Hirsch, using the more modern terminology
which stresses a Messianic 'age' rather than a personal
Messiah.

The concept of 'salvation', as applied in the Messiah, is
identical with that of 'redemption'. 'As God is the
"Moshia" (Saviour) so he is also the "Go-el" (Redeemer).'[29]
This idea recalls the Exodus experience, and links 'salvation' with 'freedom.' But this freedom is not a personal
concept. Jewish teaching is community centred. 'The
Jewish Messianic doctrine of salvation does not centre

in personal immortality . . . the Jewish saviour was not a go-el in the sense that he took upon himself the blood-guiltiness of sin incurred by another . . . the go-el never was the vicarious victim.'[30]

The Messiah will be *tzaddik*–righteous. This is seen as not simply an innate quality of character, but more a vindication–he will be 'shown to be in the right–vindicated in the face of opposition.'[31] It is easy to see how, following this interpretation, it was tempting to fit Judas Maccabeus into the frame. But the Messiah will also, undoubtedly, be humble–coming as the prince of peace (Isaiah 9:6); 'not like a worldly conqueror riding on a war-horse . . . but in humility riding on an ass, the animal used for peaceful purposes.'[32] This is not because he is compelled to poverty, 'for behold, the whole world shall be in his power, but from humility he will ride upon an ass.'[33]

Ben Maeir,[34] writing as a Messianic Jew, commented on the word *nosha*, rendered in the NIV as 'having salvation'; the implication being that the Messiah will come bringing salvation as a benefit to others. He pointed out that the word is an adjective and should be translated as either 'helped' or 'saved.'

> The Messiah needed the help of the Father all along the way. He needed the Father's support to execute his duties as saviour of Israel. In Psalm 22, which the suffering Messiah repeated from the Tree, there is a loud cry for salvation. 'Save me from the mouth of the lion' (v.21) . . . the Messiah needed help, prayed for help, and the Father gave him the desired help. Therefore, is the Messiah said to be Nosha.

It is Ben Maeir, again, who took hold of the word *ani* translated above as 'gentle', but more accurately 'lowly'. The word means, literally, 'poor', 'and should be literally understood . . . he (Zion's king) chose to be poor, so that by his poverty he may make many rich.'[35] So Ben Maeir points us forward to the New Testament teaching concerning Messiah. 'The Son of Man,' said Jesus, 'has nowhere to lay his head' (Matthew 8:20). Paul picked up this thought when exalting the graciousness of *Yeshua ha Mashiach Adonenu* ('Jesus Christ our Lord'): 'though he was rich, yet for your sakes he became poor, so that you through his poverty might become rich' (2 Corinthians 8:9).

Edersheim,[36] whose Talmudic credentials are hard to equal among Messianic Jews, was able to claim that 'with singular unanimity, the Talmud and the ancient Rabbinic authorities have applied this prophecy to the Christ'.[37] He even cited two Talmudic references,[38] as well as pointing to Isaiah 62:11–12: 'See, your Saviour comes . . . they will be called . . . the redeemed of the Lord.'

Christian interpretation makes much of the demonstration of kingliness coupled with humility demonstrated in this prophecy. Yes, 'a king is arriving.' The invitation is to sing and rejoice. But 'the Messiah will also come in a "gentle" or "lowly" spirit . . . One who has experienced humility, affliction, or the trial of being stricken.'[39] He is *nosaa*–'The king has been through some ordeal in which he has experienced the Lord's deliverance, and so is victorious.'[40] The donkey was not purely a beast of burden. It was also the preferred mount of princes who came in peace. The king/Messiah will enter Jerusalem not on a horse, most often linked with war chariots. His *first* coming will not be as conqueror.[41]

Here is a totally new development from the Jewish traditional one. Biblically, Christians see two Messianic comings; the first in humility and poverty, the second in triumph and conquest. Only after the second coming will the whole Messianic picture be seen and experienced: the abolition of instruments of war, 'when Messiah will proclaim peace to the nations and His realm will be world-wide'.[42] Then, and only then, will the Lord vindicate him, disarm the nations and give him dominion over the earth.

But at this first coming, as foreseen by Zechariah, the Messiah's righteousness will be plain to see. 'His nature and character will set the norms for what is lawful, just and correct.'[43] This conjunction of 'righteousness' and 'salvation' is also seen in Isaiah 40–55, those chapters which contain the 'servant songs' seen by many as Messianic. The suffering servant fits the picture of one who has suffered, experienced God's 'salvation' and vindication, and is the bringer of that salvation to others.

Palm Sunday

Jesus knew his Scriptures. He was well aware of the impact of his actions on that Sunday before Passover. He was, in fact, making a statement: 'This is Who I Am.' 'It behoved Him so to enter Jerusalem, because He was a king; and as king, to enter it in such a manner, because He was such a king.'[44] And so, recognising–perhaps only wistfully–to some degree the identity of this man, the people, ever looking and longing for the Messiah–identifying that Messiah with 'salvation' as they saw it–ran out to greet him with the festival cry: '*Hosha'na*! Save us we beseech thee, O God!' Of course the familiar words of Psalm 118; the 'salvation psalm', sprang to their lips at this festival time: 'O Lord, save us . . . Blessed is he who comes in the name of the Lord' (118:25–26). What more natural than that the bringer of God's salvation–redemption–should appear at Passover, the festival of God's salvation–redemption–from Egypt?

They were excited. Jesus was realistic, knowing what was in people's hearts, what lay ahead; his own need of God's 'salvation'-support, all other failing. Edersheim expressed it beautifully: 'He alone was silent and sad among this excited multitude, the marks of the tears He had wept over Jerusalem still on His cheek.'[45]

Salvation–the Jewish view

'The angel of the Lord encamps around those who fear him, and he delivers them' (Psalm 34:7). In Judaism, 'deliverance' is the primary interpretation of 'salvation'. Historically, when God has saved, he has bestowed freedom. Always, the Exodus experience is the bench-mark. The person who has been saved is delivered, safe (Isaiah 26:1). The national reference point is that 'That day the Lord saved Israel from the hands of the Egyptians' (Exodus 14:30). The Passover *Haggadah* is a reminder of and a meditation on that great deliverance.

At the *Seder* (Passover celebration) we remind ourselves that 'The Lord himself brought us out of Egypt with a strong hand, an outstretched arm, with great terror, with signs and wonders.' We raise a cup of wine to acknowledge that:

He brought us forth: from slavery to freedom,
from anguish to joy,
from mourning to festivity,
from darkness to great light,
and from bondage to redemption.
Let us therefore sing him a new song: Hallelujah!

Redemption is identified with this deliverance–with 'the national creation at the Exodus from Egypt'.[47] Based upon this historical experience, Israel, 'in all periods of trouble and danger, is always guaranteed salvation in its task of being an instrument for the recognition of God.'[48] But the application is broader than this. The Exodus story may have been about one nation, but Hertz stated that, in that 'epic account of Israel's redemption from slavery, mankind learned that God is a God of freedom'.[49] Israel must always keep sight of the fact that she is meant to be the medium for God's blessing–in this case, salvation–to all humankind.

As the years passed, survival became a preoccupation. In the Babylonian exile 'salvation now connoted the survival of the remnant, the return of the "saved" from exile; and God, in this new sense of the preserver of the remnant and the restorer of the new Israel, was recognised and proclaimed as the "Saviour" (Isaiah 45:21; Zechariah 8:7)'.[50] This 'survival' even came to seem like 'victory', so great were the odds against it. In fact, when Israel was, in the early days, frequently victorious in battle, this was interpreted as an act of salvation by God. They were 'victorious, and not by weapons of war, but by the protecting love of God' (Deuteronomy 33:29).[51]

So it is not surprising that Messianic expectation, inseparable from salvation, came to be associated with military/political deliverance, victory. The harder the times, the stronger that hope. So a medieval poet wrote, poignantly

Make haste, Lord's anointed, why are you lingering? They are waiting for you, weeping bitterly . . . Arise, Messiah, ride forth today upon a charging horse . . . for all my bones have been scattered, and not one is intact. But if you mean to ride upon an ass, my Lord, go back to sleep! If so, prince and Messiah, allow me, in good faith, to give you this advice; You had best keep the end secret and seal up the vision.[52]

An anonymous writer of a later date is less bitter, more hopeful: 'The Son of David will come suddenly to set his glorious flag upon the holy Mountain . . . The Prince whom you seek will, all of a sudden, come to his Temple; but he will come riding upon an ass; he sets no store by the strength of a horse.'[53] Slotki saw this victory in wider than national terms. Commenting on Isaiah 45:21, he said: 'All mankind will ultimately find salvation in God unto whom "every knee shall bow." He is the only source of strength and victory.'[54] The Messianic expectation is 'also of ever-lasting peace and the turning of all nations toward the one God of Israel.'[55]

Salvation is also 'shelter', 'security'. 'He delivers them from the wicked and saves them, because they take refuge in him' (Psalm 37:40). Cohen comments on this verse: 'God is an impregnable citadel, and they who take shelter in it survive the attacks made upon them, however bitter and prolonged.'[56] ' The Lord is . . . a fortress of salvation for his anointed one' (ie 'Messiah') (Psalm 28:8).

The one who comes bearing, or having, salvation will be humble. Humility is also to be the mark of those who receive God's salvation. 'When men are brought low and you say, "Lift them up!" then he will save the downcast' (Job 22:29). 'So long as Job is humble, God will come to his help when the arrogant try to overthrow him.'[57] This salvation, protection, deliverance, of the poor and weak is a recurring theme in the Psalms, as in Psalm 12:5: '"Because of the oppression of the weak, and the groaning of the needy, I will now arise," says the Lord. "I will protect them from those who malign them."'

Salvation is entirely an act of God, but it requires our response. It can be limited by our rejection of him (Isaiah 59:1–2); it is to be found as we return and remain in him (Isaiah 30:15). It is useless to look for salvation in other directions, 'to images of their own manufacture'.[58] But in Judaism this belief takes a different path from that in Christianity. Response is so important as to be all but cause. 'Salvation is attained not by subscription to metaphysical dogmas, but solely by love of God that fulfils itself in action. This is a cardinal truth in Judaism.'[59] One is reminded of James' teaching that faith must be seen in works. Judaism sees the Christian doctrine of salvation by grace through faith as 'easy grace', unworthy of a holy God.

There is less use of the word 'salvation' in connection with atonement, or forgiveness, than in Christianity, although that theme is prominent in the liturgy for *Hosha'na Rabbah*. But a very early writer recalled the atmosphere of tension and uncertainty in Temple times on *Yom Kippur* (the Day of Atonement): "Give us a sign," they say to him [the High Priest], by which we shall know that our sins have been atoned for.' Whereupon he shows them the messenger who despatched the goat [scapegoat]; he bears tidings of salvation.'[60]

The 'good news' more usually hoped for down the ages has been that of comfort, of relief, release from the present intolerable situation. 'We longed for your salvation as one sighs for the shade, as a servant pines for his wages,' comes a cry from the eleventh century. 'We hoped to hear good tidings: "The Redeemer has come!"'[61] And, a century later: 'Lord, thrust exile into oblivion . . . Your salvation is my heart's desire. Oh, bring it now to your weary and languishing people.'[62]

The Crusades were an age of terror for Jewish communities, as 'Christians' saw no reason to spare one set of 'heretics' on their way to tackling another! 'What can I hope for? My wound is as huge as the sea. Who but you can ease my pain, O Healer of all suffering? On the day when I hear the voice that bears good tidings, I shall bow down and prostrate myself. I shall rejoice greatly when my Ransomer, the Mighty One of Jacob, cries aloud: "Comfort ye, comfort ye my people!"'[63]

Sometimes, understandably, there has been a sense that the waiting has gone on too long–as, for instance, in the years up to and including the twentieth-century Holocaust. 'Had I come too soon, or was the Rock, my Creator, late?'[64]

Hoshi'a-na is the heart's cry of a people in pain; a long scream echoing down the ages. Ages punctuated by two events of colossal significance: 1) The incarnation of *Yeshua*, who came 'to seek and to save'; 2) The Holocaust, leading to the establishment of the State of Israel–a people once again rising out of the ashes. But now, at last, no longer content to cry 'help' and wait, they have determined to take their destiny into their own hands.

Salvation–the Christian view

The New Testament word 'salvation' derives from the Latin *salvare*–'to save', and *salus*–'help', 'health'; also from the Greek *soteria*–'cure', 'recovery', 'redemption', 'remedy', 'rescue', 'welfare'. It is 'the action or result of deliverance or preservation from danger or disease, imply-ing safety, health and prosperity'.[65]

The Christian view, broadly, is that the whole Bible, both Testaments, is an unfolding of God's plan for the salvation of fallen humanity and, indeed, of the whole creation, which is also suffering as it awaits the final redemption (Romans 8:18–25). This salvation is to be primarily from sin and its effects. Men and women as individuals need to be saved. Society needs to be saved. Creation needs to be saved. This salvation was accomplished in Jesus on the cross, and attested by his resurrection. 'It is in the death of his Son that God performs the focal act of salvation for man.'[66] It was, therefore, absolutely appropriate that the Messiah should be given the name *Yeshua* (Jesus)–'God is our salvation'.

The cross was a cosmic event, with effects beyond the reach of time and space. This means that salvation is seen as past, present and future: 'He has delivered us . . . and he will deliver us . . . He will continue to deliver us' (2 Corinthians 1:10). Nevertheless there is an undoubted individual dimension to New Testament salvation. Perhaps sometimes this dimension is over-emphasised, but it cannot be denied. God saves a community. God saves men and women, you and me.

Salvation operates entirely by the grace of God. 'It is by grace you have been saved, through faith–and this not from yourselves, it is the gift of God–not by works, so that no-one can boast' (Ephsians 2:9). This is a cardinal doctrine of the Reformation. 'Nothing in my hand I bring–simply to thy cross I cling.' 'If there is to be any salvation for either Jews or gentiles, then it must be based, not on ethical achievement but on the grace of God.'[67] What must I do to be saved? Paul replied: 'Believe in the Lord Jesus, and you will be saved' (Acts 16:31). Peter expressed it more fully: 'Repent and be baptised . . . in the name of Jesus Christ for the forgiveness of your sins . . . the promise is for . . . all whom the Lord our God will call' (Acts 2:38–39).

Salvation: from–sin and bondage; into–freedom and life; for–'whosoever.'

Notes

1 *The Jewish Encyclopedia* (Funk and Wagnalls Co., 1903).
2 Rabbi S.M. Lehrman, *Sukkoth* (A Bachad Fellowship Publication, 1943), p.23.

3 *Ibid.*, p.12.
4 Succ.48b.
5 Succ.53a.
6 Succ.4:5.
7 *The Service of the Synagogue: Tabernacles* (G. Routledge and Sons Ltd, 1904), p.173.
8 *The Jewish Encyclopedia.*
9 Dr J.H. Hertz, *Authorised Daily Prayer Book* (National Council for Jewish Religious Education, 1945), p.792.
10 White burial garment. Worn on *Yom Kippur* by those conducting the services and by some more pious congregants.
11 Rabbi S.M. Lehrman, *op. cit.*, p.19.
12 Dr J.H. Hertz, *op. cit.*
13 Rabbi S.M. Lehrman, *op. cit.*
14 Dr J.H. Hertz, *op. cit.*, p.179.
15 Rabbi S.M. Lehrman, *op. cit.*, p.19.
16 Dr J.H. Hertz, *op. cit.*, p.181.
17 *Ibid.*, p.185.
18 Rabbi S.M. Lehrman, *op. cit.*, p.19.
19 *The Jewish Encyclopedia.*
20 Scholar and writer. Twelfth century.
21 Leader of the successful Maccabean revolt.
22 Rabbi David Kimchi. Known as ReDak. 1160–1235.
23 Rev A.M. McCaul, trans., *Commentary on Zechariah* (James Duncan, 1837), pp.92–93.
24 *Ibid.*
25 Soloman Bar Isacc. French commentator on Bible and *Talmud*. 1040–1105.
26 Rev. Dr A. Cohen, ed., *The Twelve Prophets* (Soncino Press, 1948), pp.305–306.
27 *The Jewish Encyclopedia.*
28 Samson Rapael Hirsch, *Horeb*, 1837 (Soncino Press, fourth edition, 1981), p.210.
29 *The Jewish Encyclopiedia.*
30 *Ibid.*
31 Rev. Dr A. Cohen, *op. cit.*

32 *Ibid.*

33 Rev. A.McCaul, *op. cit.*, p.88.

34 Ben Maeir. Twentieth-century Israeli Messianic Jew.

35 Commentary on Zechariah. Unpublished manuscript, p.71.

36 Late nineteenth-century Hebrew Christian scholar and writer.

37 Alfred Edersheim, *The Life and Times of Jesus the Messiah* (Longmans, Green and Co., 1892), p.370.

38 Ber.56b; Sanh.98a.

39 Walter C. Kaiser, Jr, *The Messiah in the Old Testament* (Zondervan, 1995), p.216.

40 Joyce Baldwin, *Haggai, Zechariah, Malachi* (Tyndale Press, 1972), p.165.

41 Walter C. Kaiser, Jr, *op. cit.*

42 *Ibid.*, p.217.

43 *Ibid.*

44 Alfred Edersheim, *op. cit.*, p.363.

45 *Ibid.*, p.373.

46 Order of service for the Passover ceremony.

47 Samson Raphael Hirsch, *op. cit.*, p.637.

48 *Ibid.*

49 Rev. Dr J.H. Hertz, *The Pentateuch and Haftorahs–Exodus* (Oxford University Press, 1930), p.3.

50 *The Jewish Encyclopedia.*

51 Rev. Dr J.H. Hertz, *The Pentateuch and the Hafturahs–Deuteronomy* (Oxford University Press, 1936), p.435.

52 Immanuel of Rome, c 1261–1332 *Advice to the Messiah.*

53 *Anonymous. Fourteenth–seventeenth centuries.*

54 Rev. Dr I.W. Slotki, *Commentary on Isaiah* (Soncino Press, 1949).

55 Gershom Scholem, *The Messianic Idea in Judaism* (KTAV Pub. House Inc., 1979), p.56.

56 Rev. Dr A. Cohen, *The Psalms* (Soncino Press, 1950).

57 Rabbi Dr V.E. Reichert, *Job* (Soncino Press, 1946).

58 Rev. Dr A. Cohen, *The Twelve Prophets*, p.49.

59 Dr J.H. Hertz, *A Book of Jewish Thoughts* (Oxford University Press, 1920), p. 25.

60 Yose Ben Yose, fourth or fifth century, *The Vestments of the High Priest.*

61 Samuel Heshelishi, c. 1000, *The Message.*

62 Ephraim of Regensburg. 1110–1175.

63 Anonynous, eleventh–thirteenth century.

64 Saul Tchernikhovsky, 1875–1943, *As I Stood.*

65 *New Bible Dictionary* (IVF).

66 *Ibid.*

67 F.F. Bruce, *Paul, Apostle of the Free Spirit* (Paternoster, 1977), p.328.

הנבי

She was a second-year student; one of that generation of 'scholarship kids' discovering the benefits–and otherwise–of the new social mobility. The price, of course, was insecurity; no longer comfortable in the old environment, not fully accepted in the new. In this rootlessness she longed for an anchor, to feel a sense of belonging. Walking one day on the Sussex Downs a sudden conviction dawned that such beauty could not have happened by chance. There had to be a 'mind' behind it. There surely must be a God. And if there was a God, he had the right to make some demands on her. Surely, God was calling to her, 'I'm here.'

An intellectual hurdle had been leaped. The spiritual search now began. She tried going to church and found that she enjoyed it. The youth group were friendly and welcoming, the services meaningful. But still something was lacking and she knew she didn't really belong. She joined the college Christian Union–somewhat unwillingly, not keen to be involved with 'that bunch of nuts'. Gradually she was being drawn in deeper from the security of the sidelines. At a conference the search culminated in discovering the words of a young man who, centuries before, heard the voice

of God saying, 'Whom shall I send? And who will go
for us?'

'Here am I. Send me!' replied Isaiah.

It was time for her to say, 'Here am, I Lord–*Hineni*.'

12

HINENI
הנני

Often my husband, when he'd been out, would call as he came through the front door, 'Darling! Where are you? Up or down?' And I would answer, 'I'm here–in bed,' or, 'I'm here–in the kitchen,' or wherever I happened to be. He was asking because he didn't know where I was and he wanted to locate me, to be with me, to share his day with me. So my answer gave him the information he needed; told him something he didn't know; reassured him. I was waiting for him, glad when I heard his call, ready to respond.

Now, plainly, when God calls people he is not asking for information because he knows very well where we are. When he called to Adam in the garden, 'Where are you?' he wasn't enquiring about location. He was asking Adam to face up to something and stop trying to hide. He was reaching out in love, longing for a response, ready to repair the broken relationship: reminding Adam–'I'm here.'

The literal meaning of *hineni* is 'behold me!'.The older translations of the Bible would use the word 'lo'. So, for example, Isaiah's response was rendered 'Lo, here am I'.

The lexicon[1] defines the meaning of this expression as 'an indication of the readiness of the person addressed to listen or obey'. We can learn more about *hineni* by looking at some of the different ways it is rendered and used in the Scriptures, in order to understand better the implications of responding to God in our own lives.

Here I stand

In 1 Samuel 12:3, Samuel's farewell address, the prophet said, '*Hineni.*' He called upon the people to testify against him if they could. The NIV translates it as 'Here I stand'. Samuel was challenging them to find fault with him, claiming that his life was an open book. So here *hineni* means, 'I'm hiding nothing from you.' Not to be open like this is to be to some extent a hypocrite. And some of Jesus' harshest condemnation was for hypocrisy. How many of God's servants are one hundred per cent what we appear to be? And doesn't the world know it! Isn't there a crying need for Christian leaders who can say, '*Hineni*–here I stand, hiding nothing. Condemn me if you can.'

Behold, we are your slaves

In Genesis 50:18, Joseph's brothers threw themselves at his feet with the words, 'Behold [*hinenu*], we are your slaves.' They were saying that they had no claims on him and he had the right to do absolutely anything he wanted with them. He could destroy them–as they deserved, or he could accept, restore and provide for them–an act of unmerited graciousness. Similarly, in Joshua 9:25, the Gibeonites said to Joshua, 'Behold [*hinenu*], we are now in your hands.' They had practised deception and been found out. What could they do but throw themselves on Joshua's mercy, acknowledging their utter helplessness, worthlessness. The words, 'I have the right' are out of place on the lips of servants and dependants, particularly when they are never spoken by the master! '*Hineni*' means, 'I have no rights; the rights are all yours; I am utterly dependent on you–at your mercy.'

Here we are before you in our guilt

In Ezra's day (9:15), the priest's representative prayer of contrition included these words: 'Behold (*hinenu*), here we are before you in our guilt.' The people, newly restored to the land, had sinned crassly, the leaders and officials having led the way. Ezra had sat in mourning and self-abasement and prayed, 'Oh my God, I am too ashamed and disgraced to lift up my face to you' (9:6). There was an acknowledgement of sin and a desire to know how to rectify the situation. How much better for Adam in the garden if he had responded, '*Hineni*' in this sense when God called, instead of hiding and then making excuses (Genesis 3:9–10). '*Hineni*' can mean, 'I know I'm in the wrong. No use trying to hide it. I'm ashamed before you. Please put me right again.'

What can I do?

The young man who brought David the report of King Saul's death related how the king had caught sight of him after the battle and called out to him. Then he responded, '*Hineni*.' It is translated in the NIV as 'What can I do?' Someone to whom you owe allegiance calls you, needs you. Things are going badly; you seem to be on the losing side. It could be risky, dangerous, to stay around. But your instant response is to express readiness for action. 'Tell me what to do, and I'll do it' (2 Samuel 1:7). '*Hineni*' can mean loyalty when the going gets rough.

What do you want of me?

Think of Moses. God came to him in person–so he plainly knew where he was!–and called him by name. 'And Moses said, "*Hineni*."' Of course he wasn't saying, 'I'm over here, Lord.' He was expressing availability. 'I'm here, Lord. What do you want of me?' All right, he had a bit of an argument with God when he found out what was going to be expected of him, realising the enormity of the task and the scale of the cost. But the intention was right, and the basic expression of readiness. The rest would eventually follow. Without that initial, ungrudging response of '*Hineni*', he would never have stayed the course. '*Hineni*' means total commitment; nothing held back. 'I know I'm not up to this, and you know I really don't want to do it. And, frankly, I'm terrified. But because you are my God and I am your servant, I'll do it, come what may.'

I'm here, Lord

Then there was Samuel again–just a child; too young to know what he was doing, you might think. Certainly he was too young to realise the full implications of what he was doing when he obeyed Eli and responded to God with the word, '*Hineni*.' But did he understand much less than Moses had before him? Can anyone realise the cost, the pain, the loneliness, that may follow the initial response to God? I certainly didn't. How many of us would have started the journey of faith if we had known the future? Thank God we didn't! So why discount the response to

God of children? I too am a child when it comes to understanding the ways of God in my life. '*Hineni*' can be the start of something truly significant, as it was with Samuel. Without that unreserved response at the beginning of his life how would he, a mere child, have been able to grasp the nettle of relaying God's words of judgement to Eli the priest? And how would he have been able, as an old man, to say to the people, '*Hineni*–find fault with me if you can!'

I am grateful for those from whom I learned, at the beginning of my Christian life, that following Jesus is an 'all or nothing' matter. Total commitment–consecration–is required. We do people no favours by presenting Christianity as an easy option; 'Come to Jesus and all your problems will be solved.' Let us not be afraid to issue the challenge as Jesus himself did. He did not say, 'Follow me and life will be a bed of roses,' but, 'Follow me and I will make you . . . .'; 'Come to me and bear my yoke.' Perhaps there would be fewer disillusioned Christians, fewer 'drop-outs', if all new believers were taught to say, '*Hineni*' right from the beginning.

Here am I. Send me

Back to Isaiah. He was given an inkling of the cost very quickly after saying, '*Hineni*.' God laid it on the line: 'Go and preach to this people–but I know they won't listen to you.' When many preachers hear the call to ministry, surely we dream of large congregations and noticeable response. We think wistfully of Peter's first sermon, of Billy Graham. And that is how our success is rated. 'God really blesses his/her preaching' means, 'Lots of people respond to his/her preaching.' Success is seen to be the hallmark of God's approval and blessing. To put it crudely: blessing = success. But Isaiah was a failure according to that criterion. So '*hineni*' can mean, 'I'm even prepared to be a failure in everyone's eyes if that's what you want; to feel at the end that I've accomplished nothing, been of no influence whatever.' Now that is really costly, particularly nowadays.

Isn't it true that contemporary judgement is hard on what it sees as failure? And we hate failure in ourselves. Think about it. Who do we hold in honoured memory? Isn't it those who 'made a mark', achieved something measurable? But a clear call like Isaiah's may not necessarily lead to what the world, or even the Church, would call successful ministry. There are no guarantees here. We write a blank cheque when we say, '*Hineni*' to the Lord.

I trust you, Lord

Abraham was called upon to say, '*Hineni*' in the most extraordinary circumstances. Twice he is recorded as saying this word in Genesis 22. He was an old man now, who had walked with God and been his friend for many years. Of course he responded readily to the voice he knew and trusted (v.1). It might have been just like me answering my husband's call. But no. When God dropped his bombshell: 'Take your son, your only son, Isaac . . . and . . . sacrifice him,' Abraham showed that he was not just saying the words, not even just enjoying the relationship, but expressing a trust that is almost beyond belief. As he proceeded to carry out this act of obedience and faith, he was *still* listening, *still* responsive. We know this, because we read that when 'the angel of the Lord called out to him from heaven, "Abraham! Abraham!"' (v. 11), he replied, *yet again*, '*Hineni*' (v.11). Abraham trusted that God would be true to his past promises and, indeed, to His own nature. He did not know *how* it would work out, but he knew it would. This unshakeable trust was expressed in that one word–'*hineni*'. '*Hineni*' means that we will trust God with what is most precious to us. We will trust him when nothing seems to make sense and we haven't a clue what's going on in our lives; when his ways are totally incomprehensible and it is difficult, oh so difficult, to trust.

Even my reputation, Lord

It was a young girl called Miriam who had the most startling encounter of them all. She, legally betrothed but not yet married, was to become pregnant by God's Holy Spirit and give birth to the expected Messiah. She would believe it, but who else would? What would this do to that good man, Joseph, her betrothed? How would he react? Could he be expected to cope with being derided as a cuckold? What of her family, the community? Would they throw her out? Oh, the misunderstanding, the condemnation, the shame! 'Behold,' she responds. 'I am the Lord's servant' (Luke 1:38). The language is different, but the idea is the same: a humble, submissive acceptance of God's will for her life. In such a culture, at such a time, a young girl's most precious possession–the one treasure that, however poor, she would be expected, and would herself expect, to bring to the bridal bed–would be her virginity, her honour. In today's culture it is difficult for us, perhaps, even to begin to understand what was being asked of her and what she unreservedly offered. But in any society, any community, reputation is highly valued; the esteem of family, peers and social circle is not lightly jeopardised. '*Hineni*, Lord–even my reputation.' What a challenge!

Yes, Lord

A man named Ananias appears in the story of the conversion of Saul of Tarsus (Acts 9:10–19). 'The Lord called to him in a vision, "Ananias!" "[Behold me]," he answered'. 'Yes, Lord. I'm ready, Lord. Just say the word and the answer will be "Yes".' We never hear of Ananias again; one of the Bible's 'little' men–not particularly notable. He was only given one job that we know of–and he argued about that! But when he obeyed, he did it whole-heartedly, even to addressing Saul, the enemy, as 'Brother Saul'. And his 'hineni' transformed the known world! He was needed to get Saul going, to complete the conversion process. Don't let us ever think that our response or lack of it is of no importance because we see ourselves as 'little', insignificant.

We have no way of knowing our own potential. The future is hidden, and God's plans for us far beyond our vision. But one thing is certain. If we are to be what God wants us to be, and do what God wants us to do, the first step must be to say, 'Hineni–Yes, Lord' to him; assured that God, for his part, will never fail in his response to us when we call, when we are in need, when we obey.

Behold me, trembling

There is a prayer known as Hineni which is a silent meditation used by the Reader in synagogue services, immediately before the recital of Musaf–the 'Additional Prayers' which were inserted long ago to take the place of the Temple sacrifices. It is the cry of a man who feels unworthy in leadership, but desires not to fail his people. He lays himself open to Almighty God and to his mercy:

O Lord, who inhabitest the praises of Israel, behold me, poor of good deeds, trembling and terrified in dread of Thee, I have come to plead before Thee for Thy people Israel, who have deputed me; although I am not worthy of it. Hence, I beseech Thee, Thou who art the Almighty God, the faithful and most High King, accept my prayer which I offer with my whole heart favourably, O Thou who art the only living God, who art the true and just Judge, merciful and gracious, have mercy upon me, and hear my prayer which I offer this day for myself, and for my congregation, who are in concord with me in prayer, and include my prayer among the perfect and pure prayers offered by the House of Israel, and suffer not those who have deputed me to be put to shame through me, nor I through them.

May the words of my mouth and the meditation of my heart be acceptable in Thy presence, for the sake of all those who were righteous, pious and upright, and for the sake of Thy glorious and revered Name. For Thou in mercy dost hear the prayer of Israel Thy people. Blessed art Thou who hearest prayer. Amen.

The God who says, '*Hineni*'

Isaiah (65:1) tells how God himself promises that when this rebellious people do eventually turn and call on him, he will reply, '*Hineni, hineni.*' The repetition of a word in Hebrew is to give emphasis. But you can see that here again is the basic meaning–that of response. When God calls us, we often keep him waiting. But when we call to him, he responds readily, whole-heartedly, emphatically.

Jesus, supremely, said, '*Hineni*' when he came to do his Father's will and give his life that we might be reconciled to the Father. 'Here I am,' he said (quoting Psalm 40:6–8), 'It is written about me in the scroll–I have come to do your will, O God' (Hebrews 10:7). This offering of himself was never easy. We can discern the struggle from the temptations through to Gethsemane. Can any price, therefore, be too high for us?

Surely I am with you always

Is it wrong to see '*hineni*' implied in the words of what we call 'the great commission' (Matthew 28:20)? The old translations used the word 'Lo' here–'Lo, I am with you always'. Isn't Jesus saying, '*Hineni*–behold me–with you always, as you go out and make disciples. Look at me; this is what I am like–the God who is here, always, for you.' Our '*hineni*' is only ever a response to his '*hineni*'.

Here am I, standing at the door

Summed up in these words (Revelation 3:20) are the constant love of God for a wayward people; the determined plan of God that he *will* live among and within them in covenant relationship; the patient readiness of God who waits on the outside saying, 'I'm still here.' He is longing to respond to a people who will turn to him, welcome him into the centre, wanting nothing better than to walk in his ways–a people who will say to him, '*Hineni*.'

Notes

1 *Lexicon of the Old Testament* (Brown, Driver and Briggs).

BIBLIOGRAPHY

The Authorised Jewish Prayer Book (Singer) (Eyre and Spottiswoode Ltd., 1957).

The Hasidic Anthology (Charles Scriber's Sons, 1934).

The Holy Bible, New International Version.

The Jewish Encyclopedia (Funk and Wagnalls Co., 1903).

The New Bible Dictionary (IVF).

A Rabbinic Anthology (Macmillan and Co., 1938).

The Sabbath (Joint Emergency Committee for Jewish Religious Education, 1943).

The Service of the Synagogue (Routledge).

Siddur lev Chadash (Union of Liberal and Progressive Synagogues, 1995).

The Zohar. The textbook of Cabbalism, a medieval Jewish sect.

Abrahams, Israel, Roth, Cecil, ed., *Jewish Life in the Middle Ages* (Edward Goldston Ltd., 1932).

Apple, Raymond, *Companion to the Machzor for Rosh Hashanah and Yom Kippur* (United Synagogues Pub. Committee, 1964).

Baeck, Leo, *The Pharisees.*

Baldwin, Joyce, '*Haggai, Zechariah, Malachi*' (Tyndale Press, 1972).

Maeir, Ben, *Commentary on Zechariah* (Manuscript, mid twentieth century).

Brown, Driver, Briggs, *Lexicon of the Old Testament*.

Bruce, F.F., *Paul Apostle of the Free Spirit* (Paternoster, 1977).

Cohen, Rev. Dr A., *Everyman's Talmud* (J.M. Dent and Sons Ltd, 1937).

Berachot (Oxford University Press, 1921).

The Psalms (Soncino Press, 1950).

The Twelve Prophets (Soncino Press, 1948).

Edersheim, Alfred, *The Life and Times of Jesus the Messiah* (Longmans and Co., 1883).

Epstein, Rabbi Dr Isidore, *Step By Step in the Jewish Religion* (Soncino Press, 1958).

Freedman, H. *Commentary on Jeremiah* (Soncino Press, 1949).

Friedlander, Rabbi Michael, *The Jewish Religion* (Shapiro, Vallentine and Co., 1922).

Ginsberg, Louis, *Legends of the Bible* (Jewish Publication Society, 1992).

Green, Arthur, *Jewish Spirituality* (SCM Press, 1988).

Haffkine, W.M., *A Book of Jewish Thoughts* (J.H. Hertz) (Oxford University Press, 1920).

Hertz, J.H., *Commentary on Deuteronomy* (Oxford University Press, 1936).

Commentary on Exodus (Oxford University Press, 1930).

Commentary on Genesis (Oxford University Press, 1929).

Hirsch, Samson Raphael, *Horeb*, 1837, Soncino Press, fourth edition, 1981). An exhaustive analysis of Judaism.

Jacobs, Rabbi Dr Louis, *Theology in the Responsa* (Routledge and Keagan Paul, 1975).

Hasidic Prayer (Schocken Books, 1975).

Jewish Law (Behrman House, 1968).

Jeremias, Joachim, *The Central Message of the New Testament* (SCM, 1965).

Jocz, Jacob, *The Covenant. A Theology of Human Destiny* (Eerdmans, 1968).

Kaiser, Walter, Jr, *Toward an Old Testament Theology* (Zondervan, 1978).

The Messiah in the Old Testament (Zondervan, 1995).

Kimchi, David, trans., A. McCaul, *Commentary on Zechariah* (James Duncan, 1837).

Klausner, Joseph, *Jesus of Nazareth* (George Allen and Unwin Ltd, 1925).

Landman, Leo, *Meddianism in the Talmudic Era* (KTAV Pub. House Inc., 1979).

Mackintosh, William, *Gleanings from the Talmud* (Swan Sonnenschein, 1905).

Magonet, Rabbi Jonathan, *A Rabbi Reads the Psalms* (SCM, 1994).

Marshall, I. Howard, *The Epistles of John* (Eerdmans, 1978).

Myers, Isidore, *Gems from the Talmud* (Simpkin, Marshall, Hamilton, Kent and Co., 1894).

Plaut, W. Gunther, *The Torah – A Modern Commentary* (The Union of American Hebrew Congregations, 1981).

Polano, H. *The Talmud* (Fredrick Warne and Co.).

Reichert, V.E., *Job* (Soncino Press, 1946).

Reinhart, Harold, *Sifre Torah* (CCJ 1964).

Sacks, Rabbi Dr Jonathan, *Tradition in an Untraditional Age* (Vallentine, Mitchell, 1990).

Scholem, Gershom, *Origins of the Kabbalah* (Jewish Publication Society, Princeton University Press, 1990).

Slotki, I.W., *Isaiah* (Soncino Press, 1949).

The Jewish Sabbath (F.O.M. Publication Co. Ltd).

Smalley, Stephen S., *1, 2 and 3 John* (Word, 1991).

Steinsaltz, A., *The Talmud – Reference Guide* (Random House, New York, 1989).

Temple, William, *Readings in St John's Gospel* (Macmillian, 1945).

Zangwill, Israel, *Dreamers of hte Ghetto* (Heinemann, 1898).

INDEX